To Diane & Fred
Great Sandy Springers!
Eva Galambos

A Dream COME TRUE

My Very Good Life

EVA GALAMBOS

The First Mayor of Sandy Springs, Georgia

authorHOUSE®

AuthorHouse™
1663 Liberty Drive
Bloomington, IN 47403
www.authorhouse.com
Phone: 1-800-839-8640

First published by AuthorHouse 3/16/2011

ISBN: 978-1-4567-4881-4 (e)
ISBN: 978-1-4567-4882-1 (dj)
ISBN: 978-1-4567-4883-8 (sc)

Library of Congress Control Number: 2011903623

Printed in the United States of America

Forewords

"…her neck stiffens and she lowers her chin…"

She is the most remarkable lady I have ever met. Fearless-dedicated-and when appropriate, always challenging statements of others, but when all the facts are before her, she is willing to accept and agree, or state valid and coherent arguments regarding what she sees as deficiencies in one's position. Her comments are never personal, just aimed at reaching the truth. Always the truth.

It is never-and I must repeat- never about her. Because she is devoid of ego, she is so capable of getting others to accept the position she puts forth as a course to follow. It's usually, "If Eva feels this is what we should do, then let's do it".

I made the decision in 2000 to seek elective office as a state legislator, and part of the district included the panhandle of what was known as "Sandy Springs Planning District" by Fulton Country government.At that time it was an unincorporated area of the county.

I didn't know Eva Galambos, but knew her to be a strong advocate for incorporating Sandy Springs (which at that time was a pipe dream). It was explained to me by several supporters that Eva was someone you wantedon your side.It so happened a mutual friend of ours, anartist, was having a showing of his art work in his home, and let me know Eva and her husband, John, would be attending. Well, I made certain Vicki, my bride, and I would be there, as this I felt would be important for my political career.

Eva was a most engaging and charming lady. It was apparent Eva wanted to know who I was, andmy position on various issues, especially on city hood for Sandy Springs.I fully supported the effort, and that started what became a fastfriendship (which grew stronger over the years).I won my election due in large part to numerous friends and supporters Eva persuaded to vote for me.

For many years a bill had been introduced by the Representatives of Sandy Springs for its incorporation. It was, shall we say, DOA,and notlikely to see the light of day. We perfunctorily always signed our names to the bill, and I did so without actually reading the bill, knowing it wasn't going anywhere. As one legislator said in opposing city hood, "Sandy Springs will become a city when pigs fly", which became the mantra for the movement (in fact, Eva's mayoral office is decorated with flying pigs found by friends from all over the world). This attitude was a norm until the "revolution" which occurred in 2004, when the Republicans became the majority party in the state House and Senate, along with a RepublicanGovernor. All of a sudden, I said, "Wow, I need to read this Sandy Springs bill" it has a real chance, now, of passing. So, in preparation for the 2005 legislative session, all involved began to seriously study the bill and steps necessary to see its implementation to bring about the incorporation of Sandy Springs.

This involved not only a Charter Bill, but also major revisions in other general laws which effected incorporating a new city. Throughout this endeavor the steady leadership of Eva, and her passion, kept us moving to the eventual goal--making Sandy Springs a reality. At each step of the process from drafting bills, holding hearings and debate on the floor of the House and Senate, there was Eva overseeing the progress, offering encouragement and guidance to us all.

The legislation all passed; we were on the way to becoming a city, but first we had to ensure this was what the citizens wanted, so a referendum, required by law, was scheduled. Eva spent endless hours in meetings with groups explaining the benefits of incorporation andwhat this would mean for the community.

To no one's surprise, really, it passed, but few could conceive of a margin of 92% approval. The people had spoken, and they wanted a city. Eva was the overwhelming choice to be the city's mayor, and although she had opposition, she won by over 82% voter support. That, I would say, is a mandate. Her leadership made possible Sandy Springs, and chartered the course for the unbelievable tasks which faced all, becoming a city of 90,000 people in less than thirty days from election to start up, December 1, 2005. Her leadership as Mayor was validated, when in 2009 she was re-elected by an even greater margin.

In this wonderful life story you will be amused reading of her outlook on people and how she sees things through her innocence, which she still has to this day. But pity the individual who thinks her a fool and tries to get something past her with loose facts. As I have observed her over the years she is quick to point out deficiencies in a position when it lacks substance. After years of working closely with Eva it is easy to know when she has made a decision. Her neck stiffens and she lowers her chin to her chest. What usually follows is a compelling statement of whya position lacks sound reasoning and why she can't support it. With Eva decisions are never personal; never malicious-just fact based.

What Eva has accomplished as mayor is nothing short of amazing. Over 90 miles of streets paved; 9 miles of new sidewalks; establishment of a new police department with over 120 officers, and a fire/emergency rescue department, the finest in Georgia. The list could go on and on. The future of our city is bright and promising, due in large measure to the dedication and leadership of the one we call affectionately, "Queen Eva". Hers is truly a very good life as it has brought so much good to her community, and, as in the movie, we are to wonder what Bedford Falls would have been without George Bailey? Well, I wonder what would Sandy Springs be (if at all) without Eva Galambos?

Wendell K. Willard, Georgia State Representative, District 49

"…many would have given up—but not Eva!"

As Assistant Dean of Women at the University of Georgia in the mid 1940's, my job was to work with the outstanding women students. Eva Cohn Galambos was certainly outstanding, not only in academics (Phi Beta Kappa), but in extra-curricular activities as well.

Eva and I both met our husbands (her father, Dr. Sigmund Cohn, was one of my husband's professors) at the University. When she and I both married and moved from Athens to Atlanta, our friendship—now including husbands and children—continued to grow. And after sixty-four years, it has become one of my most treasured possessions.

I was impressed by how Eva balanced her life by always putting her children and husband first, even while pursuing her PhD and working for the southern Regional Education Board (SREB). This effort was rewarded in later years by the wonderful relatiopnships she now enjoys with her accomplished children (two doctors of medicine and a PhD graduate in physics), six grandchildren and a blissful marriage of over sixty years to Dr. John Galambos, one of America's preeminent gastroenterologists. They joyfully supported her and delighted in her many accomplishments.

Eva's persistence continues to impress me to this day. She spent countless, long hours on the marble floors of the Georgia Legislature lobbying for the citizens of Sandy Springs to have the right to vote to become an independent city. After many frustrating years attempting to accomplish this goal, many would have finally given up—but not Eva! When her dream was finally realized, the people of Sandy Springs voted overwhelmingly to incorporate, and soon after they elected Eva Cohn Galambos as their inaugural mayor. In 2010, at the age of eighty-two, she is serving her city—now Georigia's seventh largest—for a second term. Remarking that many elected officials declare a "landslide" when they receive fifty-five (or so) per cent of the vote, a local columnist recently wondered what Eva's whopping eighty-four per cent reelection margin might be called!

I have always thought Eva's life—from escaping the Nazi terror in Germany to her arrival at the University of Georgia in Athens—to be most remarkable. I am delighted that she has chosen to write her story.

Marth Latimer Young, Atlanta,Ga.

Contents

Prologue

My life in this country began when I arrived on the Italian ocean liner REX. Most of the ship's passengers were, like me, refugees fleeing Europe. I came to this country with a spattering of English in 1939. My husband, John, came in 1947 with ten dollars in his pocket. Now here we are, enjoying another whole chapter of life with me as mayor of Sandy Springs and John as "first man." We are meeting more friendly folks and having a ball. We've raised our own family of three children and are watching the progress of six grandchildren with interest. Four have already graduated from fine universities. Our financial future is secure. We are not vegetating, but, rather, are savoring the challenges and daily events of each week.

I read the diaries of my grandmother and father shortly after each died. I can't say that the diaries of my family really motivated me to start on this project, but they did fill in background for the beginning of my own story. While I was reading my grandmother's diary, I was instantly struck with the *joie de vivre* which characterized her writing. She exuded warmth in person, and it comes through in her writing style. My father's writings, meanwhile, were much more historical than personal, delineating the many events that took place simultaneously with the personal happenings. My grandson Daniel, who majored in history at Lewis and Clark University in Portland, Oregon, took my father's diary as his project in research based on authentic source. He tied all the narrative to the happenings in the background and produced a new version of the diary, which documents the history of the period on one side and the personal narrative on the other. He even unearthed the manifest of the ship we all traveled on and found our names on it.

This record, meanwhile, was written at various stages of my life and reflects that, whenever I wrote, I thought I had arrived at the end of the narrative. New pursuits or events have continually transpired, however, that have spurred me to update and continue my story.

I've divided this version of my story into two parts. The first part, "Once Upon a Time," is my recollection of the events of my life, what some would say is a most American story, even though it begins in Germany and Italy. The second part, "One Long Day at a Time: Making the Dream Called the City of Sandy Springs Come True," is a detailed account of an important part of my life and a significant chapter in the modern-day history of Georgia.

This project started as a way to evaluate how I got to where I was. Sometimes the adventure and mystery of it all strikes me as rather dramatic, as when I was inducted as an honorary member of the Sandy Springs Chapter of the Daughters of the American Revolution. I almost could not avoid writing my story, even for my own sake (and certainly for my children and grandchildren and in honor of my parents and grandparents). I'm interested in history and biography and enjoy seeing how the twists and turns in people's lives—and my own—add up to become the present. I often ponder the effect of the strange choice to study labor and industrial relations in 1948, for example, and the repeated choices not to pursue legal studies. In the final analysis, however, these don't really matter. When I am asked to talk to young folks about how I prepared for my present role, I cannot lay out a direct route. All I can say is this: Life is a series of crazy twistings and turnings, but if you try to do the best at every turn, it will work out okay.

E. G.
Summer 2010

Part One
ONCE UPON A TIME

Berlin and Sunny Italy

1928-1933—Berlin, Germany

My maternal grandmother, Regina Sternberg Lewy (Oma), was a constant in my life from the beginning—she was jolly, loving, and my sister and I could do no wrong in her sight. She attracted people, she loved good food, and she was always able to see the bright side of life. She was quite attractive with grayish-green eyes and high cheekbones. She wore her straight hair pulled high on her head with combs to hold stragglers in place. She often wore dark dresses with white lace collars.

She was born in Ostrovo, in what was then Germany but reverted to being Poland after World War II. She grew up in a small town, but was well educated by tutors and local schools. When she was sixteen, she was sent to a girls' boarding school in Berlin. She writes in her memoirs that many young men followed the girls home from school, but the chaperones chased them away. There were large families of numerous aunts and uncles, however, which engendered lots of gatherings where eligible young partners could meet. She met her own future husband at one of those gatherings and noticed that he was pleasant and seemed to be well educated. Grandmother liked interesting people and always enjoyed jokes, so I imagine her husband must have been entertaining as well.

Max Lewy, her husband, was the son of Louis Lewy, Jr., the owner of the largest department store in Breslau. My grandparents went on a grand tour for their honeymoon. My grandmother was very close to her father, who cried when she departed on the trip. They began in Vienna, and then on to Venice. She was scared in Venice at first, because they arrived late on a winter evening, when it was already dark. That time of year there were no tourists, and she was alone with the gondolier while her husband looked to the luggage. They traveled in winter and summer, because fall and spring were the busy seasons in the store.

In Venice they stayed at the Hotel Danieli. I visited it when we were there as tourists in 1975. It was still a very ornate and swank place. We stayed next door, in what was a somewhat less expensive but also a highly decorated hotel, with lots of engravings and embroideries throughout the suite.

My grandmother writes of the glorious sun shining the next morning in St. Mark's Square. She fell in love with Venice then and maintained that feeling for the rest of her life. A guide showed them works of art and the sights of Venice. He also accompanied them to the stores to buy gifts and then to a fine restaurant for lunch. She writes that she realized, in retrospect, that he probably got a fine commission from every place they shopped. They attended the opera, and marveled at how loud and enthusiastic the Italian patrons were in comparison to the more sedate Germans.

The next stop was Nice, on the Riviera, with the blue Mediterranean on one side and the fields of blooming flowers, violets, carnations and roses for miles and miles in every direction, and the mountains in the background. Their afternoon entertainment was to parade along the Promenade Des Anglais, where their hotel was located, and to "people watch" from cafes. They proceeded to all the famous resorts: Sanremo, Bordighera, Menton, Cannes and Monte Carlo. The people in light clothes with bronzed complexions presented a sharp contrast to the people they had left in Germany. In Monte Carlo they gambled for a short time. Their Riviera stops included Cap-Martin and Cap-Ferrat where they indulged in drinking coffee or listening to music in the sun. Homeward bound, they stopped in Milan to see the famous cathedral and the Leonardo da Vinci mural there, *The Last Supper*. She remembered the opera at the Scala—*Lucia Di Lammermoor*. The final stop was Pavia, where they viewed an old cloister with works of art, and went shopping to buy presents for every member of the family at home.

They returned to Breslau from their month-long honeymoon to find a totally furnished apartment. Every piece of furniture and equipment was in place, including a grand piano, down to the "toothpicks and matches." Her in-laws had prepared it all.

Upon her husband's death at the end of World War I, my grandmother inherited considerable wealth, which enabled her to live well. During the horrendous inflation in Germany after the war, however, her memoirs describe the daily struggle for food, as inflation reduced the value of currency each day. By the end of this economic cataclysm, shoppers were wheeling the worthless currency around because it was too bulky to carry on one's body. One of the important stamps Dad would show us in his collection was a German one: "See," he would point out, "the original value has been stamped over with lots of zeroes for the millions to show the new price."

Even in the difficult post-war years, when my grandmother was trading rooms in her home for butter from a renter's farm, she traveled. From resort to resort, in Tuscany, Switzerland, or the Riviera, down to Naples and Sicily, repeatedly to her favorite Venice, and then on to Yugoslavia, vacations and traveling were part of the annual routine. Everywhere there were cafes and lovely restaurants with memorable wines. For fun, there was people watching and shopping for gifts to bring home. Wherever she went she recalled the operas she saw, the famous art she viewed, and the innumerable new acquaintances they met in the hotels along their itineraries.

The acquaintances and friendships she made while traveling turned into correspondences. Postcards later arrived from all over the world and became part of the stamp collection I kept in those days. Some of the stamps are from colonies, which are now independent countries. My father's beautiful stamps from countries all over the world, meanwhile, were an introduction to geography and to countries that were created after World War I. Recently I passed this collection on to the grandson who completed a BA in History at Lewis and Clark University in Portland, Oregon. He seemed quite interested in the collection, despite the fact that it was very incomplete.

My parents were both born in Breslau. My father, Sigmund A. Cohn, was invited to my uncle Walter's twenty-first birthday party, which is where he met my mother, Susan. He writes in his memoirs that it was a costume party. The guests were supposed to wear something to signify their future calling. He wore a judge's robe, since he was heading into the legal field, but apparently was mistaken for a future rabbi.

Shortly after that party he, Walter, and some other young people, including my mother, went on a three-day hike. He found her open, sweet, caring, and unaffected. They clicked, and courted for some time, mostly by going on hikes and to concerts or operas.

I was five when we left Germany for Italy, so I remember very little of life in Schmargendorf, a suburb of Berlin. My younger sister, Marianne, and I lived with our parents in a grey apartment building among many more just like it. I remember that we had a maid who helped Mother with such things as watching us and carrying coal from the basement up to the central stove to heat the apartment. There was a back garden cut into small plots for the various households. In the garden, I had a chance of meeting other children to play with. There was a gooseberry bush laden with fruit that I sampled when I somehow escaped the Nanny's supervision to join the other children in a fruit raid, which led to serious punishment.

We shopped almost every day. There were no big grocery stores, so Mother went out every day to fetch various items from separate stores nearby, and we went along for the outings, a chance to see the world.

I had a blue winter coat with a shoulder cape that Father decreed should be removed because it seemed too pretentious. Father was structured and strict, after all, while Mother indulged Marianne and me. Eventually Dad softened and later, when my sister got a coat like mine, she was allowed to wear it.

Until the end of our time in Germany, our grandparents lived in Breslau. As toddlers, Marianne and I went on visits to our maternal grandmother's house. Oma, our grandmother lived in a much larger establishment than our apartment, and she loved all kind of houseplants, including cacti. They would be brought indoors to survive the long winters in Germany and carried out again in the spring. Once I fell from the window and landed half a floor below in the outdoor cactus bed. While the circumstances of the fall are fuzzy, even to this day I can feel the prickles as I lay on my stomach with Mother and Grandmother tweezing cactus spines from my bottom.

I do not believe we had any religious life in Germany. Many German Jews were very secular, like my family. My grandmother's father was religious, but that was where it ended. My grandmother even had Christmas trees as her children were growing up.

1933—Berlin Railroad Station, Leaving Germany for Genoa, Italy

The excitement and thrill of a train ride for three-year old Marianne and me transcended the grown-ups' anxiety as they departed their mother country before the new regime would arrest and deport them. Father, as a Jewish judge, was one of the first fired from his job, which was a lucky early warning to get out.

The cavernous station had rows and rows of platforms with trains belching smoke. When would the big engine pull up? Which was the right platform and train carriage? How to get so many suitcases on board before the train would leave? Would some be lost? We had some twenty pieces of luggage with us at the Berlin station when we left for Italy. My father would later write in his memoir: "This gave little Eva no small trouble. She counted incessantly to see whether everything was still there." Then I was ensconced in the upper bunk of a train compartment, with a bird's eye view out the window. "Will the train start before Mamma gets on?" I worried. On the platform relatives were hugging and crying as they said their last good-byes.

Our maternal grandmother and her son were scheduled to join

us soon in beautiful Italy, the romantic country of Grandmother's honeymoon and her many subsequent vacations. Our father, however, was leaving his elderly parents behind, for which he would suffer pangs of guilt for many years to come. The best memory of this grandfather, whom I almost did not know, were the paper animals that had moveable body parts. Giraffes and lions that sprang out of picture books came from his printing business. They were cherished gifts.

Later my father spoke often of relatives who disappeared as Germany exterminated the Jews, but he grieved silently for his parents. Although my father claimed that they died in some nursing home far from home where they received no care, a printed genealogical account of the family indicates they perished in a concentration camp—Theresienstadt in 1942, which would be three years after my family left Europe.

He never once again set foot on German soil, despite the fact that my parents vacationed in Europe for many years. He absolutely hated Germany, and that hatred seemed to extend to Germans in general. My father was left with two young children and a young wife and was shut out from his profession and his homeland. His feelings of insecurity throughout later life were no doubt a reflection of suddenly finding himself jobless, and then immigrating to another country where he also was officially excluded from his profession because he was a foreigner.

Genoa, Italy 1933-1939

The view from the penthouse apartment was of Mt. Righi to the east and the port of Genoa to the west. At night the mountains to the east twinkled as the lights came on at dusk. It looked magical to Marianne and me. During the day, meanwhile, we could watch the procession of freighters and steamers as they departed the port for the Mediterranean.

The apartment was large enough to accommodate Grandmother and our family plus visitors. Bachelor Uncle Walter soon joined us. We lived in the apartment with Grandmother and Uncle Walter until he was married in 1938, and my grandmother bore a good bit of the financial burden. Somehow she had managed to liberate much of her finances out of Germany, although how she did this remains mysterious to this day. Father and Walter were mostly gone during the day, although it would be inaccurate to say they went to work. At the beginning, they were looking for work. As lawyers, both my father and uncle studied to pass the Italian law requirements and sought work in law firms. Children have antennas, and I became aware that my father was frustrated in trying to earn a living for us in Italy. I am sure that living under the same roof with his mother-in-law, particularly when she was partially sustaining the family, grated on his nerves. My uncle was able to make some business connections eventually, which helped his own financial situation, and probably further increased my father's insecurity about finances. Work did come to the apartment in the end, but to my mother, not my father. Mario Podesta took German lessons from her, and the jokes reinforced the impression I got that this Italian gentleman had fallen in love with Mother.

My mother was endlessly the mediator, trying to keep everything pleasant between everyone. Neither my mother nor grandmother cooked, so every meal was dependent on the servant. My father joked that mother and grandmother stayed busy thinking up things for the maid to do.

Because the maid did the cooking, there were often Italian dishes new to our taste buds on the table. Pizza with an anchovy sauce was a highlight. A memory lingers of us in the corner of the kitchen as live lobsters were dunked into huge pots of boiling water. "Watch out, they're trying to get out," I screamed in delighted and horrified excitement.

The maids introduced us to the saints. As we took walks into the hills, there were often shrines to this or that beautiful saint, with flowers in a vase at the side. Maria collected elegant engraved cards picturing the various saints. Gradually Marianne and I started our own collections, which we compared and traded:

"I'll swap you Santa Margherita for Santa Stephania."

"No, that one has more gold trim than the one you want to swap."

Maria not only cooked but also did all the laundry and ironing by hand. The irons were heavy black-metal affairs that were heated on the stove. Maria would test the heat of the iron by tapping it on her forearm, and once she burned herself terribly. We were all aghast and worried as she continued to wear a big bandage for a long time.

When we were sick, the doctor only came to the apartment as a last resort. Usually, we were treated with our parents' home remedies first. Most of these remedies involved terrible smells. One consisted of wrapping our chests with a heated pack of towels that had been soaked in mustard. For sore throats, wet, hot towels were applied to our necks and then wrapped tightly with woolen socks. Some kind of chamomile tea was boiled, and we had to inhale the fumes with towels over our heads to form a kind of tent over the kettle. The worst was an occasional spoon of castor oil. For the most part, we were quite healthy, aside from the usual children's diseases.

Trams provided transportation everywhere, whether for shopping, hikes, or other excursions. We did not know about cars, except that we saw them occasionally on the streets. The greatest excitement, then, was when some visitors came with a car, and included Marianne and me on a ride along the Riviera coast. I remember it as a large shiny, black touring car, with a high back seat where we sat.

Uncle Walter meanwhile could always be trusted to provide special treats. He took us to a town eatery that served toasted sandwiches—a new sensation for us. At that time, Uncle Walter became engaged to Hilde from Frankfurt, whose wealthy family had also left Germany. The wedding took place in a large Genoa hotel with a lovely fishpond among the palms and oleanders. Marianne and I were the flower girls and wore pastel organdy dresses for the fancy proceedings. Favors included sugarcoated almonds wrapped in white netting. The day must have been hot, because somehow we both ended up in the pond, much to the chagrin of our grandmother.

We could take a funicular, an inclined railway, up into the mountains. Usually it was a family expedition, with both our parents along. We thought it was quite an adventure, since the only other vehicle we ever rode was the tram. Its grating was quite loud, and it made several stops from the bottom to the top, picking up customers. At the top of the funicular there were some gelato vendors. From there, paths led through walled villas and then past simple farms to the open fields. The walled enclosures around villas and farms on the lower flanks of the mountains were scary. Big dogs barked as we walked past. "Let's walk faster, Mamma," I urged in my discomfort about the unseen dogs behind the walls. Mother packed some refreshments to have as a picnic—hard-boiled-egg sandwiches, fruit, and cookies. Years later in the United States, she packed the same snacks for my children.

The Sunday walks into the fields of the mountains to the east were opportunities to gather stock for our imaginary flower shop. We could pick spring flowers of all hues and heights until we tired of the fun. Back home, after a long hike, we separated the bunches into categories for the flower shop. We gathered wildflowers: daisies, blue cornflowers, and what were probably weeds, but we thought that our bunches were gorgeous. We arranged them in various combinations and pretended to sell them to the doll customers. The open terrace, with primary-color glass panels surrounding the apartment on two sides, was a wonderful spot to pursue endless imaginary games like the flower shop. Of course, all our make-believe conversations were in Italian, which seemed to be our mother tongue for many years.

The glassed veranda of the Atto Vannucci apartment was also the chosen site for afternoon tea, over which Grandmother presided. She was a commanding and jolly presence, and set the tone for meals and servant behavior. The veranda was usable about nine months of the year, until the weather was finally too cold. Then the scene shifted to the inside dining room. There was always a nice tablecloth and Grandmother's Limoges china, and the children were allowed a treat after a proper curtsy and introduction. She liked to live on a fairly grand scale, and she remarked in her memoirs that everything was cheap in Italy, so it was easy to live well.

As to the teas, there was a constant flux of visitors, usually speaking German, who visited with Grandmother and, of course, Mother. (They were people who had also emigrated from Germany.) On our veranda, they swapped countless tales about who had gone to which countries, how they earned a living, who married whom, how their children were faring, when they were last seen. The international situation and what was happening in Germany were the foremost topics of conversation.

My grandmother had lots of relatives, but also a huge retinue of acquaintances. She was charming and full of energy and stories, and people flocked to her. When she traveled, she made friends in the hotels and pensions where they stayed, and kept in touch with each other after they had returned home. How all these people corresponded with each other so frequently before all our modern communication technology still amazes me.

As emigrants from Germany touched base with the family, they would bring us surprises, such as huge, hollow-chocolate Easter eggs, with intricate sugar flowers and other sugared decorations. A rattle gave proof of a surprise inside the egg. It was a major decision whether to break the egg and taste it or save it because it was so beautiful. On one occasion, when Marianne's fell and broke, I had to swap mine with hers:

"It's not fair, why do I have to?"

"You're the older one and she's so little," Father reprimanded me.

The grown-ups had long, serious discussions with these visitors. They probably centered on everyone's future prospects and on this and that person left behind. We were vaguely aware of terrible events in Germany and that Father anguished about our grandparents left behind in Breslau. Yet these problems only affected us children indirectly, when our parents were too distracted because of their worries to respond to our demands for attention. Yet these tensions do not predominate in the memories of growing up in a warm household and the experience of going to school.

At school, we concentrated on drill after drill to perfect basic skills and handwriting. I think we were segregated by gender, with boys and girls in separate classes. We had endless rote learning. At the beginning, perfect handwriting was stressed *ad infinitum*. Marianne somehow always forgot that the margin was not be transgressed, and this lapse earned her demerits. There was much less self-expression in the Italian curriculum. When we drew a picture, it was of an assigned subject, so we all drew, basically, the same picture. Prayers were part of our school day, too. The family was regaled at Christmas by our recitation of the poems about Baby Jesus that we had dutifully memorized at school. Between radio broadcasts about the terrible events in Germany, the family that had gathered to hear the news would indulge us with applause as we proudly recited the Christian poems taught in our public school.

Someone must have realized the irony of our reciting Christian prayers when we had left Germany because we were a Jewish family. So Hanukah lights were introduced at some point. Yet the memories of the Jesus prayers are much clearer today than those of the Hanukah ceremony. After all, we were a family to whom such religious observance did not come naturally.

We wore uniforms to school, white shirts and dark skirts. Eventually, the young fascist uniforms were added to our wardrobe. We learned all the patriotic songs, marched, saluted, and generally went along with what the other children were doing. We showed off at home, to parents who were far from pleased, I'm sure.

In 1938, the dilemma of Jewish girls doing fascist salutes was resolved when Mussolini decreed the schools would not allow Jewish children to attend. I missed the other children, but our education continued as the teacher, who had little sympathy with the Fascist decrees, came to the house and brought the assignments. Nobody was to work for Jews any longer, either, and so the maid had to go. The postman came by, and missing Maria, asked incredulously, "You really let her go?" The average Italian was not supportive of the Fascist decrees, but since Mussolini had to obey Hitler, the handwriting was on the wall.

One heard *Il Duce* incessantly. He was praised in the schools, and there were many parades in which school children participated. He spoke (although it sounded more like shouting) from the porch of a government building in Rome on many occasions. I never saw this in person, but the speeches were played on the radio. We never sat around the radio listening to him. None of the family took *Il Duce* seriously, but the fact of Hitler's increasing domination over *Il Duce* was becoming clear, and, thus, the necessity for our family to leave Italy. Also, the danger of war was ever closer after Prime Minister of Britain, Chamberlain, caved in to Hitler in Munich.

During the summers, we swam off the rocky beaches of the Mediterranean. A walk led to the tram, and then another from the end station to the beach establishment, where canvas dressing cabins were available to rent for the season. We spent endless hours climbing rocks, searching for crabs between the cracks, and collecting bright fragments of broken bottles, which accumulated into treasured collections. The waves battered the fragments so they were rounded, and the green, brown, amber and rare blue shades seemed like jewels.

Somehow, we learned to swim, without any more instruction than our parents gave us. Lunch was brought from home, and in the afternoon, tired from an active day in the water and sun, we struggled to the tram, often falling asleep on the ride home.

Special excursions on Sunday, often led by Grandmother, took us to Nervi, then a serene suburb of Genoa. A promenade atop the sea-cliffs meandered around the curves, with the sweet aroma of yellow mimosa overpowering everything else in the spring. The highlight of the excursion was the stop at the ice cream vendors. "I want a gelato limone, per favore," we asked while eying the assortment of flavors.

The summer seasons in Italy always included a mountain trip. The family rented accommodations in the Italian Alps in one or another village, where hiking excursions were the daily entertainment. One such village was Macugnaga, an undiscovered spot high in the meadows with vistas of the snow-covered Alps. The locals anticipated the annual appearance of a small circus troupe, complete with dancers, jugglers, and some sad-looking donkeys. During the day, one could glimpse the performers in their rickety trailers, looking after their children and going about their lives. At night, they were transformed into troubadours, as they offered to a totally enthusiastic audience folk songs and opera excerpts performed with all the Italian pathos they could muster. Then the hat would be passed to receive the few pennies the natives could spare and the occasional larger offerings from tourists.

Many years later, when the Italian movie *La Strada* came out, it had a particular emotional tug for me. I had personally witnessed such itinerant performers in tatters.

The exception to our general good health was that I contracted whooping cough before one scheduled summer vacation. The concerned family kept trying to shush my coughs lest we be ejected from the rented quarters in the mountain village. Afternoon excursions culminated with strawberry-and-whipped-cream treats, which softened the fact that I was unable to join in the family outings.

Not much was clear to me or my sister about one particular summer trip to the Alps late in our Italian sojourn, when we took a circuitous trip to reach a remote Swiss village. This included a train transfer in some tiny station where two railroad lines intersected. The travel arrangements for Grandmother, Mother, and the two of us children were reviewed over and over before departure, so that even I was totally aware of the train transfers and schedules we were to meet. Many years later I understood that Grandmother had money sewn into her corsets, to be taken over the border to Switzerland at a spot known for weak surveillance. Grandmother made several trips, trips discussed by the grown-ups in hushed tones. She would somehow return from these absences with fabulous frankfurters, which were a rare delicacy for our table.

By September 1938 when we took a trip to Geneva, we children understood the situation more clearly. Before departing, all the family belongings were packed, ready for the movers, although I have no idea now as to where they would have been sent. In Geneva, we stayed in a beautiful inn full of families like ours. All the grown-ups were glued to the radio, listening to events in Munich. "Be quiet, this is important," they would shush us as they motioned us to move away. They had no more energy to spend on us; this left the younger set free to play roving games through the extensive park grounds surrounding the inn. The tension and agony of the adults did little to interfere with childish games. I now have no idea who these playmates were or where they went. Our time in Geneva ended as the Munich Crisis was resolved, at least temporarily. Chamberlain had given in to Hitler, postponing war.

We returned to Genoa and unpacked. Yet Marianne and I were now aware that we would be leaving Genoa eventually.

A tutor began coming to the house to teach us English. The talk about who would get visas to what country was constant. Important letters were sent to America, and Father made trips to consulates, government offices, and steamship headquarters.

Before leaving Italy, our parents took us to Rome and Naples. When I returned to Rome twenty-five years later, a few of the sights awoke memories. St. Peter's Basilica with its vast plaza was engraved in my mind, as was the Quirinale, and the Forum. The gaudy Vittorio Emanuele monument made an impression since we had often heard *Il Duce* on the radio making speeches from the building that faced this monument. My impressions of Naples, which we visited for some official papers, consist mainly of images of poor people on the sidewalks, people rumored to live in caves.

In 1939 the family would not all leave Italy together. Grandmother would be going to Palestine, to live with her sister. Grandmother's birthplace, the determining factor of what United States immigration list one would land on, was in Ostrovo. After World War I, this became part of Poland. The rest of the family was on a list emanating from Germany. Thus Grandmother's entrance into the United States would have to be delayed until her turn came up on a very crowded roster.

Uncle Walter and his family (which now included our one-year old cousin Renata) would also come to the United States, but on a different steamer. The family spent the last week together in some lovely hotel on the Riviera. Since the amount of money that could be taken out was severely limited, it made sense to spend it before leaving, and Grandmother always knew how to choose delightful spots. She was the one, after all, with the bleakest prospect—she would be far away from her children and grandchildren who were immigrating to the United States.

As she prepared for the separation, she also disposed of her household furnishings. The twenty-four place setting of Limoges was displayed on the grand piano, on which she had taught me to read notes and my first pieces. Strangers came and picked their purchases as the household was reduced to what would be useful in America. Of course at the time I cared nothing about Limoges—though I now treasure the delicate coffee cups and saucers that I still have, but felt vaguely uncomfortable about the loss of the piano. Grandmother had studied piano as a young girl and was quite proficient. She was familiar with all the operas and in her many travels had enjoyed performances by the major musical artists of the time. It was a given that her granddaughter would learn to play the piano.

Father had secured support to become a college professor at the University of Georgia. The impending turmoil and insecurity of another emigration must have weighed heavily on the adults. They kept their worries from Marianne and me, however. The only outward manifestation of their anxiety regarding the move was their unsuccessful search in reference materials to learn something about their future home—the small town of Athens, Georgia, U. S. A.

Growing Up in Athens, Georgia

The Crossing, February 1939

The Italian super ocean liner, REX, was a wonderful place for children. Deck after deck, everything was new and exciting—fancy dining rooms, chandeliers, an exercise room, elevators, and the stateroom. Mother and Father were ill from the passage, and their incapacity allowed Marianne and me quite a bit of freedom to explore the ship.

Apparently Mother recovered sufficiently to attend the Captain's dinner. We were led into the deepest innards of the ship to pull our velvet party dresses out of the trunk in storage.

One memory of our arrival in New York at Ellis Island is especially clear. We stood in long lines inching toward a cubicle where our eyes would be examined. I was apprehensive, because I had overheard my parents discussing beforehand that people with runny eyes were turned back. "Are my eyes okay, Mamma?" I pestered her over and over again. Would we all pass muster? Apparently we did, and we exited from the cavernous hall to claim the many suitcases and trunks that were to accompany us to some middle-priced hotel in New York City for a brief stay.

Our destination in the United States was Athens, Georgia, where father had found a teaching post through the auspices of a Jewish refugee organization and Harold Hirsch, a prominent Atlanta attorney and general counsel for Coca-Cola. (The University of Georgia's law-school building is named for him.) Because the state of Georgia forbade expenditures for non-citizens, Hirsch put up the money for two years' salary at the university. This was a time when generous Jews throughout the country reached out to see what they could do to save the Jews in Europe. On the way to Athens from New York, we went to Atlanta first because my father wanted to thank Mr. Hirsch personally. Unfortunately, he was out of town. He died two or three weeks later from a heart attack, so my father never had the chance to meet him.

Mr. and Mrs. Max Michael took us under their wings and met us at the train station in Athens. Our temporary domicile was the Holman Hotel. The Michael family invited us often to their house, which seemed like a mansion to us. They especially liked Marianne with her crown of ringlets. Dinners in the Michael home were served by kindly black servants who passed around strange dishes like sweet potatoes topped with toasted marshmallows. They delighted in asking us many times, "What are those sweet rolls with the hole in the middle?" They would roar with pleasure as we said "ducknuts." Our sparse English at that point did not go far enough to translate doughnuts into the proper pronunciation.

The different foods were quite noticeable—corn bread; soft, white loaf bread; greens; beans with fatback in them; and, of course, marshmallows. The food was so different from the crunchy bakery bread and the variety of cold cuts in the Italian grocery stores to which we had been accustomed. While we had eaten pizza quite a bit in Italy, I wouldn't have pizza in the United States until the 1960s.

Communication at that point was comical. Our parents spoke German to each other. Marianne and I conversed solely in Italian when we arrived, but shortly after being put into school, we switched to English. Before long, the Italian was dropped at home as well, and gradually our queries in English were answered in English by our parents.

In Italy, I would have been in the fifth grade, but in Athens I went into the sixth, partly due to the success of the rote-learning approach I had experienced in Italy. Junior high school in Athens consisted of the seventh and eighth grades. High school was ninth through eleventh. As the first foreigners in Athens, we were like animals in the zoo. I was invited to visit various classrooms in the school. My English did not embarrass me. People were nice. For some reason an Italian blouse made of synthetic material became a prop for show and tell. Perhaps the product hit Italian markets earlier than the United States.

Some things in school were certainly new. American history was a far cry from Garibaldi and Mussolini. But math and Latin came easy. "Nominative" and "predicative" had been drilled in Italian grammar instruction and the Italian and Latin words were often almost the same. The Roman conquest of Gaul seemed interminable to me as kids struggled with the words. To pass the time I would play games with the teacher, long suffering Ms. McWhorter. I would act as if I were asleep, in the hope she would call on me, so I could then fool her—I did know the place in the book and the translation. But I believe she was on to my game.

Until we could rent a house, we observed American life from the Holman Hotel. One of the strange things Marianne and I noticed was the same yellow car driving endlessly on the streets. Only later did we learn about cabs.

Occasionally, we would be allowed to attend Saturday matinees at the movie theatre on Broad Street. The theatre on College Avenue showed the first-run movies, but the Broad Street house catered to children and showed cartoons on Saturdays. A memorable part of these Saturday expeditions was the walk down Broad Street to the theatre. Black adults and children sat on the curbs and lingered before storefronts of businesses that catered primarily to them. As whites traversed, the blacks would step aside and make room, even for children. Apparently this was natural, as none of our acquaintances commented on the situation. Yet as a European transplant, I was vaguely aware of something disturbing. These were the days of total segregation, with dual schools. The only black people we knew were the servants in the homes. They and their families lived in old, run-down houses on unpaved streets and dressed in the hand-me-downs of their employers. When we walked the streets in the summer, we could smell the sweat from the dawdlers on the street corners.

The first house we rented was on Lumpkin Street, a half a block past Five Points. It was a bungalow with a small front porch, a screened side porch, and three bedrooms. It had a living room, which also served as my father's study, and a dining room and kitchen in the back. A botany professor used to live there; his plantings covered the property. The backyard was ablaze in the summer with blue cornflowers and other blossoms we could not identify.

When the furniture arrived in huge crates, there seemed to be a lot of interest from passersby. Strangers assembled to watch a huge moving van discharge the massive European furniture, with the wardrobes and buffets—so different from what most homes used in Athens. Skis were a sensation. As we unpacked and settled into the bungalow, we were delighted to find Oma's home-baked panettone hidden in the buffet. It made the ocean passage safely in its tin and was just as good as when she baked it months ago.

For our birthdays, Mother tried to reproduce our favorite dishes. Although she had never really cooked in Europe, once in Athens, she was determined to learn. My request for a lemon chiffon pie must have been the supreme challenge. Although Mother had a clerical job at the University and also went to school for years as well to qualify for a teaching certificate, she did not assign many household duties to Marianne and me. It was "Do your lessons," or "You haven't practiced the new Mozart piece, and you have a lesson in two days!" Our responsibilities were academic, not household related.

Mother had occasional cleaning help—provided by an elderly black lady named Birdie. She was also our baby sitter in those early years when our parents were invited to some function. Poor Birdie was helpless against us two mischievous youngsters. We were particularly interested in the American celebration of Halloween, which was all new to us. The idea of dressing up as ghosts was instantly appealing. When our parents left, as soon as darkness fell, Marianne and I donned our sheets and escaped to the yard. Then we proceeded to howl and scare Birdie. Little did we know then about the significance of white sheets to black people. Birdie was petrified, and although Birdie continued to help our mother, our parents had lost their babysitter.

Grandmother, who had immigrated to Palestine because she was on the Polish quota for entry to this country, finally obtained her visa in 1942. After spending three years with her sister in Tel Aviv, she boarded a freighter and sailed around the tip of Africa to join her children in the United States. She told fascinating tales about the assortment of international refugees on the ship and about waiting in the darkened freighter as it avoided unfriendly encounters. As always, she made friends with everyone, including some of the crew.

Grandmother's trunks contained unlikely treasures, such as a collection of ostrich feathers, which had once been in great fashion. She gave them to Birdie, who wore them to her Sunday services. When I was married, Birdie appeared at the synagogue dressed in her white uniform adorned with the ostrich feathers.

When Grandmother joined us after her detour in Palestine, she was delighted with the new house since the screened porch was enveloped in the early spring by a huge wisteria vine, which was one of the botany specimens. Its lavender blossoms, with a sensuous fragrance that seemed almost obscene, were new to all of us, and cause for annual anticipation.

Summer vacations were long and languid. The heat in Athens was something new to us, and, of course, nobody had air conditioning. There was no air conditioning anywhere except at the movies. My mother suffered from the heat and would spend afternoons on the recliner just trying to get through the worst part of the day. As the older child, I was assigned the task of cutting the front lawn with a hand-pushed, reel mower. On a typical July day, I would come in limp and exhausted by the end of the job.

During the torpor of the summer months, I read my way through the shelves of the Athens Public Library in the era of the great contemporary novelists. The library was about at the corner of Lumpkin and Broad Streets where the Holiday Inn is today, as best I remember. I checked books out of the library, and brought them home in the basket of the bike. (A bus came down Lumpkin Street, which I might have caught sometimes, too.) I did not spend much time in the library reading. I liked to curl up at home to read. First, in junior high school, I devoured Nancy Drew stories and anything by Zane Gray. Thereafter, I read through the twentieth century British and American novels, such as Steinbeck, Thomas Wolfe, and Hemingway and all the great fiction writers of the time. The entire family read *Gone with the Wind*, which I think my parents had read before we came to the United States. My parents never objected that anything might be too advanced. In retrospect, sex education was a side effect of this reading, and not the focus of any family talks.

We had more freedom to play with other children in Athens than we had experienced in Genoa. It was quite natural for the next-door kids to gravitate to our backyard and for all of us to play pretend games in what had been a chicken coop. In Genoa we had only played with other children who were brought over when their parents came to visit.

The summer camp at the Athens YMCA, then, was the undisputed highlight of our summer. It was some ten miles from town. (Now the site is well within built-up Athens.) In those years, however, the Athens Y Camp was a fairly unsophisticated affair. We swam in the "pool," which was a hole in the ground that had been partially paved, so the water had a muddy tinge. We had simple sports such as archery and softball. In the evenings we all gathered in the main-activities hall and learned many traditional camp songs and cheers and performed simple skits. When it was time to go to sleep in our bunks, we talked and giggled and gave our counselors a hard time.

We lived in primitive wooden bunkhouses with three-foot wooden walls topped with screening. Some ten to twelve girls plus counselors filled each bunk house. The food was basic Southern fare—lots of corn bread and greens. Although it was totally different from our diet at home, we thought it was good. I was never homesick or frightened.

There was a constant fear of polio, however, which was then the nightmare of families during the summer months. Our parents soon came to the camp to retrieve us because we had apparently been exposed to the disease and needed to go into a two-week quarantine. We begged our parents, "Please, don't make us leave!" There were copious tears, but to no avail.

In later years, the Athens Y Camp became the site for high school parties and proms. Once I saw prisoners with chains on their ankles who had been assigned to clean up the muddy bottom of the pool. At that time, prisoners could be hired out to work on private properties. I do not recall seeing prisoners shackled at any other times, but that one instance left a strong imprint.

The real assimilation took place as I made friends in high school. My best friends were twins—Sue and Gene. I was always closer to Gene, however, who was the really daring one. Their father was Rupert Brown, a respected attorney in town who took cases some other attorneys were loath to handle. In some ways you might say he was a maverick. I recall he ran for some kind of office at one time, and I helped the twins address postcards for his campaign.

Gene's appetite for mischief knew no bounds. In junior high school there were telephone pranks. We would dial numbers at random and would ask the answering party such questions as "Are you the lady that washes?" When the reply was negative, our response muffled with giggles would be, "You dirty thing!" Or to the drug store, "Do you have Prince Albert in a can?" (Prince Albert was a popular brand of tobacco.) When the answer was positive, we were jubilant: "Well, then, let him out!" Hours could be spent in such silly amusements, with occasional snacks of Mrs. Brown's home-baked corn bread.

The twins liked to come to our house for what they considered exotic foods. Mother always served a variety of cold cuts to make sandwiches for lunch, quite different for Athenians brought up on corn bread and bacon.

The Brown's home, meanwhile, was always an open house and their mother allowed a great deal of freedom and informality. The clique gathered there most of the time. Bicycles were our mode of transport. Without today's fancy multiple gears, we negotiated the hills with determination or simply pushed the bikes when a hill finally became too steep to ride. The Athens swimming pool, our only option for swimming, was located between two steep hills. One had to push uphill to go home, so we were sweated through by the time we made it back, having completely lost the cooling effect.

During summer, we could disappear for the whole day, visiting from one house to another, with a brown bag packed for lunch. Mother would prepare a sandwich with bologna or salami and maybe a hardboiled egg. Our hosts provided drinks. In those days we drank a lot of water; we were not addicted to bottled drinks of any kind. Of course we also had tea when we visited friends. Companionship was the main attraction, and food was the least important aspect of our outings. We were safe, and parents would not worry. In the summer, we rode to outlying areas where classmates lived on farms. Our toes would sink into the squishy mud of creeks and rivers, often in the shade of overhanging trees covered with vines. Or we would jump rocks in a fast running creek, trying to stay upright on the slippery parts. Always there was girl talk, and more girl talk.

We went to visit the twins' grandmother's farm occasionally. This was always a day trip; Gene's mother drove. The farm included an orchard of peach trees. I recall an almost fairyland-like view of endless blooming pink trees. The house was a very simple farmhouse with a front porch and rooms that led into each other. I am not sure at this point whether the house was painted. A lot of farmhouses in those days were not painted. My English teacher in my freshman year at college remarked to me once how poor the South was as compared to her Midwest, since the Southern farmers could not afford paint. I had never even noticed the lack of exterior paint until she mentioned it.

Some things we did were plain crazy. The University of Georgia football field (Sanford Stadium) lies in a natural bowl. Someone told us that huge storm sewers were placed under the center of the playing field to provide drainage.

"I double dog dare you to go under the stadium," Anne or Sue or

Gene proposed. There was no escape from a dare like that. Somehow we crouched and crawled through the dark and dank storm sewer all the way under the field. "I can't see. My knees are bleeding from the rocks. Do you suppose there are any snakes down here?" The only way out was to return the same way, groping our way gradually back to daylight and salvation.

The grassy hills of the university campus—many of them topped by buildings today—provided various opportunities for fun. During one winter marked by an unusual snowfall, we got our skis out of the storage shed and tried them out with our friends. (I had never skied in Europe, although in Berlin I did have a few ice skating lessons.) During the summer we could slide down the hills in cardboard boxes.

"How come you got Kotex boxes?" Betty teased me. I was embarrassed enough without having someone point it out.

"That's what they gave me in the grocery store."

High School in Wartime

The war affected our lives to some extent: the draft took older brothers, for example, and gasoline was rationed. But since our family didn't have a car, gas rationing did not matter to us. I have no memories of any food shortages, although I believe we had ration stamps for some items. The shortage of labor as so many young men departed did have one unusual effect on the high school: we were asked to pick cotton. The older classes spent entire days in cotton fields, where we mixed fun with work. Bending over to pick the cotton from the low bushes soon felt very uncomfortable. I sat on the sack as I dragged it down the row, slowly filling the bag with cotton. We would assemble for lunch in the shade of a huge empty barn and then bring the sack to the barn for weighing at the end of the day. We were paid a penny a pound, and good pickers ended the day with one dollar. We brought our lunches and drank the lemonade that was provided for numerous breaks, since late September or early October in the open fields was still quite hot.

Our other contribution to the war effort was to collect scrap metal. The city took up the streetcar tracks from long-retired trolleys, and the citizens scoured yards and crannies for any old metal pieces to go into the scrap collections. Never was a town so clean of metal litter.

Cigarettes were scarce, and this was significant for me because for some reason I had started experimenting with cigarettes by my senior year in high school. I recall buying cigarettes the next year, my freshman year in college, one at a time from the snack store. We all had cigarette cases in those days. In fact, cigarette cases were one of the more popular gifts for young soldiers to buy their girl friends.

We were not yet naturalized American citizens, so technically, as German citizens, we were "enemy aliens," even though we had escaped Germany. According to law, enemy aliens could not travel without notifying some government agency to obtain permission.

Father was always a stickler for the law; he filed intangible tax returns even the last year, when the law was declared unconstitutional. I pleaded, "Dad, nobody is going to care about my going to an out-of-town game." But he would not relent. So joining my friends for an out-of-town high school basketball game was forbidden. That made me different, the last thing a high school girl wants to be.

While I had friends and lots of fun in high school, there were limits to show that I was still different. In junior high school, all the girls in my crowd belonged to the social club—the Nit-wits. One had to be nominated and elected to the club. There was excited chatter at recess as one or another girl announced, "I got my invitation to join the Nit-wits." I did not make it and pretended I did not care. Nor did I make the Half-wits later in high school, nor the final accolade of the SAPS in the senior year. That left me out of the fun of proms, most of which were sponsored by these clubs. During recess and in the restroom, others would giggle and compare notes of how many entries were filled on their prom cards, while I tried to act as if it were nothing to me. (As best I could gather, these proms consisted of boys walking a girl around the block, with the party culminating in the risqué game of spin-the-bottle.)

For the most part, sports were what you picked up in the neighborhoods. Some kids had a basketball hoop, which led to impromptu games, boys and girls together. The good players would let us join as they needed to fill up their teams. I acquired the nickname "Vaca," (Spanish for cow) to describe my level of agility and skill on the court. But I was a devoted spectator at the girls' basketball games, since some of my best friends made the high school team, and I understood the nuances of the game.

Football games at the Athens High stadium were something I

attended because everyone else was there, but I never really understood the fine points of the game, and tended to get bored. Nor were the boys I secretly admired those who played football, so the glamour of watching the most "popular" boys had little appeal for me.

High school was fun because of all the extracurricular activities. I was particularly involved with the high school newspaper. I am astounded now that we managed to put out an eight-page paper every week. We had no computers, and all the copy had to be hand typed. We did our own layouts and headlines. I was one of the top editors by the senior year, and contributed many news and feature articles. Of course, the most popular part of the paper was the gossip section that described who was seen with whom. That was not the part I wrote. Our revered English teacher, Miss Ruby, was adviser to the newspaper, and an inspiration to us, as well as to prior generations she had taught at Athens High School. She and her sister, Miss Martha, were both angular and over six feet tall, with slightly hunched shoulders. Their grey hair was pulled straight back and wound into a tight knot at the back of their heads. They wore mostly black or navy blue clothing and square-toed shoes with laces. Their entire lives were devoted to teaching, and looking after a brother.

Ms. Moore, our algebra and geometry teacher, explained the theorems, and then left us to solve the problems while she knitted and knitted. Trigonometry was offered in our last year, the eleventh grade, to those who wanted it. We were well prepared for the algebra courses in our freshman year of college.

Each girl could choose between various practical courses—home economics, typing, or drafting. Most of the boys ended up in shop courses. I took typing, which turned out to be the most practical legacy of my high school years. By the time I had my first job on a newspaper, I was typing eighty words a minute, which enabled me to keep up with my thoughts much better than clumsy handwriting.

Miss Ruby instilled discipline in writing and exposed us to great literature. Her classes were a legend for more than thirty years. While

I was her student, I even took a liking to poetry, although that genre ceased to hold my interest thereafter.

Our high school building was ancient and tended to spring leaks in the roof. Then we arranged our desk chairs so as to evade the falling plaster that was loosened by the wetness seeping through. Not too many years after we finished school, the building was razed.

One of my exciting high school memories concerns a weeklong strike. We all stayed out of school to object to the board of education's decision to force our beloved principal to retire at his birthday, which was in the middle of the school year. Mr. Mell was beloved, not just by us, but by the previous generations he had taught. (Here's one example of how special he was: on field trips, Mr. Mell would whistle the birds' songs so well that they would answer.)

We somehow got it into our heads we would prevent his imminent retirement. Perhaps some parents were in the background behind this strike. In an act of civil disobedience, we paraded through the streets of downtown Athens, carrying posters announcing our cause. We even put out bulletins to publicize our position and distributed these around town. (And this was before the days of Xerox and cheap printing.) Where we got the funds to print flyers is a mystery. For an entire week we sat in the gym or paraded downtown, rather than to attend classes. And we won the point!

The most productive accomplishment of that week for me is that I learned to play bridge. As we sat in the bleachers of the gym, with cards dealt on a cutting board, somehow bridge instruction ensued. I was hooked. During college years there never seemed to be enough time to play, but I came back to it with joy in later years.

As we grew older, the amusements changed: boys, boys, boys. By 1943 and 1944 (during junior and senior high school years) Athens became inundated with the armed forces. The naval aviation cadet school was on the main campus. These were the elite boys picked to become officers and pilots. They were not allowed to ride in cars, so for a date, we girls had to meet them in town or else walk to town and then back with them. This led to a lot of walking.

At the coordinate campus (which before the war had housed freshmen women in order to protect them from the dangers of men on the main University of Georgia campus) the Army Specialized Training Program (ASTP) housed hundreds and hundreds more men. They were training to become communication and radio specialists. Their stay in Athens before being shipped to the front was short.

For Gene, this multitude of men presented unlimited opportunities, into which she led the rest of our crowd with zest. At the beginning, when we were still sophomores, she would have us camp on her front lawn on deck chairs, and notes with names and our telephone numbers were thrown to passing convoys. This resulted in telephone calls, but that was all.

As we became a little older, and the Naval cadets were judged to be gentlemen, we would attend Saturday dances or accompany these boys to the movies. Gene organized blind dates. Her contacts seemed endless. Sometimes there were not enough girls to fulfill all the blind-date demands. One memorable evening she resorted to subterfuge to meet the demand. I arrived at her house where we girls were to assemble for our dates and was introduced to "Geraldine," who turned out to be Jerry, the younger brother of one of the girls. A scarf, a skirt, and fingernail polish did a decent job of camouflage. "Geraldine" was a fairly good-looking date. What did these navy boys think of this bunch of silly Athens girls who were convulsed in gales of giggles throughout the evening? Finally, when the obligatory ice cream sodas were ordered at the drugstore, one of the Navy boys proposed we should adjourn to the nightly dance. At that point "Geraldine" got very cold feet and remembered "her" sick grandmother at home.

Gene finally confessed to her date at a later time what a terrible trick she had played. Could it be the boys really had not known already?

High school graduation was June 6, 1944, which, of course, turned out to be D-Day. This was an unforgettable combination. On the one hand we were attuned to our gala night, which in those days still meant wearing long formal dresses, with layers and layers of pastel net over hooped petticoats. Each girl was escorted to the stage by one of the male members of the class. I was valedictorian, and for once I was determined not to wear my eyeglasses. So I memorized the speech. Mother fretted, "You'll lose your place, and not be able to read your speech." But I was adamant. The speech had something to do with the responsibilities of citizens in a democratic society.

The evening was overshadowed by the awareness of the Normandy invasion, which had just begun. The boys in the class, many in their uniforms, would no doubt be leaving to join the invasion. Many friends and older brothers were already in the service. The bittersweet partying that night took place while at the same time we listened to radio news briefs about the Normandy landing.

The innocent socializing with the Navy boys, which did fill their empty evenings, was gradually replaced for me with more meaningful encounters with the ASTP boys. My high school years had produced a consciousness that, for anything more than casual encounters, my social life would be with Jewish boys. I had pined secretly for a date with Harvey, the smartest boy in the class. He was friendly, but dates with him were not in the cards for me.

Even in college it became pretty clear that while I might have some true Gentile male friends, they were not meant to be love interests. In the forties, Gentile and Jewish people led separate social lives.

The Hillel chapter in Athens provided the chance to meet Jewish ASTPs, my first boyfriends. There was Melvin, from the Bronx in New York City, whom Grandmother looked down on because he had a Polish name that ended in "witz." He liked me, however, and for the first time I felt cherished by a boy. Soon he was shipped overseas, and another soldier from Pennsylvania became my boyfriend. In his case I reciprocated his feelings. (When my granddaughters would dress up as exotic scarf dancers, they enjoyed the sequined chiffon scarf he gave me.)

He was shipped to Europe after D-Day, and we corresponded regularly. Then his letters stopped coming. For weeks I was in anguish.

Finally in January 1945 my letters came back, marked "missing."

Mother held on to these returned letters for a while, trying to spare me, but eventually the truth came out. Some time later his parents were in touch with me to tell me the sad news of his death in the Battle of the Bulge. By then, the winter of 1945, I was a freshman in college. One of the other freshmen girls had just been notified her brother had been killed in action. The entire sorority was thrown into deep gloom, as the war hit home among our very own contemporaries.

My guttural "r" was a constant reminder to me that I was not yet truly American. Strange mispronunciations from the past, which had sent girlfriends into hysterics, were no longer a problem by my freshman year. Gene used to ask with an impish grin, "Eva, how do you say that word about the reference book we use for spelling?" I could laugh with them at the way I had once said "en-cy-clo-pe-di-a," with a short "e" sound for the "cy," and with the primary accent on "di" as a separate syllable. I still suffered internally, however, because of my "r."

The teacher assigned to my section of college freshman English at the University of Georgia undertook to change this. Sylvia Schacht was a war bride with a one-year old baby and a navy husband overseas. She was lonely, and I needed help: it was a perfect match. Evening after evening I spent at her rented home near the coordinate campus. Some nights she would engage a baby sitter and join my family, who soon loved her, for the evening. Sylvia had found kindred souls, liberals interested in literature and world affairs. My parents were enchanted by her warm personality and good looks; she had heavy blond braids crowning her red-cheeked face with its sparkling blue eyes—a truly Scandinavian look.

Night after night, Sylvia used mirrors and poked toothpicks into my mouth to determine what my tongue did differently than hers in pronouncing "r," and she succeeded. Once she discovered the mechanical difference and explained it to me, I would slow down with the "r" words, and get them right. Before long the German "r" was gone—so much so that I cannot reproduce it today.

Venturing Beyond Athens

To get away from Athens, the rabbi in Athens helped me get a job as a counselor at a Jewish camp in the Poconos in Pennsylvania for the summer of 1945. This was my first exposure to Jewish traditions and practices. I loved the singing and absorbed the Hebrew songs and chants with enthusiasm. The camp was led by a reconstructionist rabbi. At the time, I knew nothing about the Jewish reconstructionist movement. My first exposure to a lot Jewish kids my age (an element missing in Athens) was satisfying. The food was unbelievably delicious—this camp also gave me my first exposure to great Jewish cooking. One of the senior counselors taught me a lesson that lasted through the years: "Always have more than enough food the first few days, so the kids won't have to fear that there isn't enough to go around."

One evening was unforgettable: Abe Goldman, a counselor from New York City, knocked at my cabin door after the kids were asleep. "Come out, something big has happened! Our forces dropped an atomic bomb in Japan!" Our wonder, our excitement, our questioning of what it all meant knew no bounds. I knew nothing about physics; I understood nothing of the science. But we knew something had happened that had changed the world.

Counselors always had one day off per week. Getting out of camp on our days off was a status symbol, and not easy to do since none of us had cars. One wild escapade was the hitchhike by several counselors to reach "civilization," (Scranton was the closest town) away from the kids. Our first ride was in a produce hauler. There were too many of us to fit in the cab. Some of the boys squeezed into the back, to emerge later smelling like cabbages. But we had still not reached our destination. The next ride was a in coal truck. Again, some sat in the back on top of coal. We were a straggly looking bunch, well before "hippies" came onto the scene.

The grand finale was sleeping in a ditch by the side of the road, when we couldn't find a ride back to camp. The next morning we straggled into camp late for duty, tired but delighted with our grand adventure.

When camp was over, I visited Sylvia in Detroit where her husband was then posted. The European fighting had ended by then, and the armed forces from that sector were rapidly returning. Melvin, my first boyfriend, had written he would be in quarantine in New York about the time my camp duties ended, but no exact dates were known. Soldiers desperate to come home to their families were held in port to make sure they were not bringing back germs.

Imagine my surprise when Melvin called in and announced he, too, was in Detroit. In retrospect, this was certainly a case of a young soldier who had suffered in combat and idealized a relationship while away. Our few days together were pleasant, but reality set in. We were not meant for each other.

The next summer I was a counselor at a camp on Lake Tiorati in Harriman State Park, New York. This camp was operated by the Jewish counterpart of the YMCA in Mt. Vernon, New York. Maury Antine, the camp director, was a social worker with close ties to an orphanage for Jewish boys. Several of these boys were now old enough to be counselors, and they were all appealing characters. I had a great time, becoming a girlfriend to two of them, in succession, during one summer season.

My Southern accent and ability to sing eased my way. I was called "Georgia," and I was suddenly popular, something I had never enjoyed with boys in Athens. I was a counselor at this camp for three summers in succession, and I came to cherish its forest haunts and lake vistas.

We were uninhibited and ambitious in pursuing new entertainments and ideas for the camp. One girl counselor was interested in drama. She produced *The Mikado* with campers and counselors. I played Katisha, and to this day, I love the melodies and words. We organized regattas, and the various bunk houses competed for best rowboat decoration. We produced Chinese junks, pirate ships, and gondolas. The counselors had a wonderful time. In retrospect, I wonder if the children enjoyed it all as much as we did.

Off-days allowed us to visit the environs, including West Point, which in those days was quite accessible to the public. After camp I stayed a few days with one of Grandmother's Salinger cousins living in what seemed a fancy New York apartment to me. On West 77th Street, with an oblique view from the window of the Hudson River, and a live-in maid always in a black dress and white apron who cooked and served— I thought I was amongst royalty. On emerging from the elevator, visitors rang the bell to the apartment and waited for the maid to open the door. It was a far cry from home.

The cousins were an elderly unmarried brother and sister, and in retrospect, they certainly indulged my erratic comings and goings. As I gradually developed friends from camp, I found more and more people to date. One date, Jack Stein, was a counselor from our camp who had decided he would volunteer for the volunteer brigade that American youth was forming to fight Franco in Spain. He had friends in Greenwich Village, the arty section of New York, and would take me there for visits. These friends lived in messy apartments with mattresses on the floor, but it all seemed terribly sophisticated to me at that point.

University professors were not well paid in those days, and Dad was also very conservative about expenditures. Perhaps as a result of two emigrations or of innate anxiety about his finances, Dad saved and saved, even in later years when there was no reason to do so anymore. The constant atmosphere of scarcity was embedded in my psyche from early childhood and molded my lifelong inclination to spend conservatively. I can recall my chagrin during college when our parents left town, and entrusted us with the money to pay off the milkman.

Marianne was invited to a social and felt the urgent need to buy a new dress for the occasion. I was appalled: "You can't use the milk money for that purpose!"

With household funds so tight, travel to summer camps required some savings on my part. Whenever earning opportunities arose, I jumped at them. First, I babysat with all the university professors' children. I brought books or homework to do after the children slept, and I invariably raided the refrigerator.

During high school I joined Gene and a few others assisting in the cafeteria lunchroom. One of our worst tricks there was to spread too much tuna salad on a sandwich, which when patted down provided a snack from the spread that was pushed out the sides of the bread.

From the time I was fourteen, I helped on the weekends and Christmas holidays at Bush Jewelers. The place was mobbed during the holidays with servicemen looking for lockets, rings. or other suitable trinkets for their girlfriends and families. Athens did not offer many opportunities for them to spend their pay, and so they blew it on presents at Christmas time.

I was able to pull out the merchandise from the display cases and gradually learned how to complete a sale. Help was scarce during the war, and the owners knew they could trust me and that I could make change. Most items were bought on the layaway system, and just before Christmas there was a wild push to pick up all the items.

During one summer I had a really boring job: to help Dr. Preston A. Brooks, sociology professor, with the newly released 1940 U. S. Census data. In those days everything was done by hand. I copied the requisite numbers from the census volumes in column after column of data, not knowing their future use. I just copied and checked to make sure the numbers were correct.

My earnings came in handy not only for the summer trips to camp, but also for eventual trips to New York to see my camp friends between Christmas and New Year's. For two years I was part of the throng of thousands at Times Square, cheering on the New Year as the neon ticker announced the time on the top floor of the Times Building. I do not recall a "Big Apple" dropping at that time. But one memory is clear—a huge advertisement for cigarettes that constantly blew huge, round smoke rings into Times Square.

We traveled by train in those years. My first escape from Athens was with two other local girls. Our first stop was Washington, and then I went on to camp as a counselor. There was great anxiety on someone's part that we would lose important items en route. So our wallets were tied into our purses with string. I believe our combs were likewise secured. We boarded the train with shoeboxes our families had packed with food. Hard-boiled eggs, sandwiches, fruit, and cookies held us until our arrival. We sat up all night, of course, as Pullmans were out of question financially, and the trains were always crowded with service personnel moving around the country.

Peggy Callahan and I relished in our first exposure to magnificent Washington, D.C. We traipsed from monument to monument, to the Capitol and the White House and the Supreme Court and the Library of Congress, and the National Gallery—we wanted to see it all. Our energy levels were inexhaustible. Both of us had family connections, which led to what seemed very glamorous stops. I had a distant cousin at the Brookings Institute. The wood paneled rooms and the chandeliered dining room impressed us. Peggy had a relative fairly high in the Department of Agriculture. He escorted us throughout that building and on to various interesting exhibits. He also invited us for a meal at a Washington restaurant, which, for two Athens girls, seemed the height of elegance.

One trip north occurred just as a railroad strike was called. I was on a train for several days, as it was shunted from track to track, waiting and waiting for something to happen. Finally, President Truman called out the armed forces to take over the railroad industry, and I eventually reached my destination.

New York City was unbelievably exciting to someone like me, from a small Georgia town. In those days there was little fear, and I rode the subways blithely from one borough to another, visiting friends from camp and taking in the sights. From Brooklyn Heights to China Town, from Mt. Vernon, New York, to the Battery—we moved around easily on nickel fares. My absolute favorite place to eat was Lindy's, famous for cheesecake. I would eat mostly at automats, which became popular in New York City beginning around 1912 and were very popular in the 1940s. One viewed a considerable variety of food items in glass cubicles, inserted a few coins, and out came the chosen dish, hot and steaming, or cold, as appropriate. One could get a good meal from a vending machine for only fifty cents.

I managed to see most of the Broadway hits during these repeated winter trips to New York. Ethel Merman in *Annie Get Your Gun* is still a vivid memory, as are two other musical hits: *On the Town* and *Carousel*. This was the heyday of musical comedies whose lyrics and melodies became widely popular. Popular music in those days, I think, was truly melodious, in contrast to today's three- or four-note themes repeated *ad nausea*. The words to the songs included rhymes and ideas, again in contrast to the minimal vocabulary of some of today's popular music, which can assault the listener with constant repetition.

Jose Ferrer in *Cyrano de Bergerac* and Frederic March in *A Bell for Adano* were among other memorable performances. So, too, were The Rockettes, dancing their way with precision across the huge Radio City Music Hall stage.

Years later, when my daughter was a teenager and I worried about her comings and goings, I realized what unbelievable freedom my parents had allowed me. At seventeen I was on my own in New York City, and my judgment about boys was not very sophisticated. Fortunately, the young men I met at camp were near my age and almost as innocent as I was. Counselors at camp went through successive intense crushes, and after the campers were asleep, there would be secret meetings and smooching and petting. But to my knowledge nobody progressed beyond certain self-imposed limits.

The moral codes and the fear of pregnancy were still mighty inhibitors for girls in the 1940s. Even in college, the exception to this prevailing attitude among my sorority sisters produced dismay and muted whispers as one girl had to leave because she was pregnant.

Higher Education

Music was an important element during my college years. I had taken piano lessons all through public school from Miss Kimbell. She insisted on perfection of a few major pieces each year. I would struggle to get these pieces right, but never mastered sight reading or understood the principles of harmony (which would have helped me with sight reading.) Those were not part of what she taught. By the time I reached college, I gradually switched from piano to voice lessons.

I tried out for the glee club as a freshman. Mr. Warner, the director, who was always on the lookout for singers for the various productions, noted my contralto. Mrs. Schinn, a voice teacher and the wife of one of the University of Georgia law professors, had taken me in tow and was determined to transform me into a singer. I vocalized and trained with her for about two years, and she talked my family into the possibility of a great talent. She even prevailed in sending me to the Curtis Institute of Music for an audition. I think Grandmother was particularly supportive of this move. The idea of a woman studying business still seemed strange to her. The audition at the Curtis Institute in Philadelphia was an ordeal that led nowhere. My talent was obviously not great enough to warrant being a voice major, but singing in a variety of operettas and taking the alto lead in Pergolesi's *Stabat Mater* added zest to college life and gave me the chance to meet a whole new group of students. At Christmastime, Mr. Warner included me in the choir to sing in the Catholic mass. I recall the rush of closing up at the jewelry store, doing my singing assignment with the beautiful Gregorian chants at midnight mass, and then taking off for New York on the Seaboard Airline train the next day.

My energy levels seem to have been high, almost inexhaustible in those days. There was the sorority, the debate club, Hillel, and the international relations club. Sorority affiliation was a given in those days. There were two Jewish sororities, Sigma Delta Tau and Delta Phi Epsilon (DPhiE). I was invited to the pledge functions of the latter, which entailed wearing dress clothes in September when the temperatures were still in the nineties, with, of course, no air conditioning. I was sixteen and overweight and had no sense of fashion. (I wore summer cottons instead of the expected fall creations for the freshman rush.) In later years I laughed when my friends told me, "We almost blackballed you because you were so awkward and unsophisticated."

The sorority initiation ritual was full of mumbo jumbo, candles, and special garments. In an overheated room, the pledges were taught the secret rituals and handshakes, with endless individual recitations of their commitments. I actually passed out from standing in one place too long.

Our social life revolved around the sorority, with its formal and informal affairs. The Jewish fraternities paired with the Jewish sororities for most of these occasions. There was practically no inter-religious dating.

Eventually I became president of the chapter, but I never lived in the sorority house. Intuitively I knew I could organize my time much better living in my parents' home than in the noisy sorority house with four girls per room. As president, I had the job of making sure the sorority house would be cleaned and ready for occupancy when the girls came back in the fall. One of the most disturbing things that happened to me, in my innocence, was to stumble on the cook on the floor of the kitchen with a man on top of her. I hastily retreated and hardly knew what to do, except to be totally confused. Not even the movies showed such activities in those days.

One of the most comical events about those years was one spring-rush weekend when high school girls from small towns throughout the state were invited to the sorority for what, to them, would be a very important occasion. Probably as a result of chicken salad, the Saturday evening turned into a disaster rather than a gala affair. Almost everyone had the runs. With bathrooms that were normally shared by four, plus the high school visitors, it was a calamity. The fraternity across the street at least was able to supply additional toilet paper. I do not know whether that weekend yielded more or fewer recruits for the next fall.

Tobae Claire Love was my favorite sorority sister throughout college. She hailed from Columbia, South Carolina, where I visited her several times. Between the junior and senior years, she decided to get a nose job in New York City. When I visited her in the hotel there, her face was grotesquely swollen, but that did not interfere with her joy of life. She insisted on ordering strange drinks from room service in her father's business suite. I spent the night there, and must have caused some gossip among his business customers. When I answered one business call in his absence, the caller inquired, "Is this Mrs. Love?"

"No, this is Eva Cohn," I blithely answered, totally unaware then of what rumors I might be starting. .

My first encounter with John Galambos was at a sorority formal dance. I was on the elevator in a formal gown, without my purse and in need of a dime for a phone call. John was on the same elevator, and produced the dime. I've been paying it back with love every since. We would have met in any event. When John arrived at the University of Georgia with his European transcripts and credits, Dad was asked to assess them for conversion into American credits. He was the one professor on the staff who could translate from various languages. In an effort to help out the refugee boys who were gradually arriving, he translated credits liberally. He knew, of course, that European educational standards had been tougher than the somewhat easygoing levels in American schools and colleges.

The Tau Epsilon Pi (TEP) fraternity house in Athens adopted John, with free housing and board, and since the TEPs and the DPhiEs were natural partners in socializing, we were destined to meet. My husband still likes to tell the story that when he arrived at the TEP fraternity and started dating me, the frat brothers counseled him to date my sister. "She's the pretty one, and Eva is just a brain." It is probably true that all through the years of schooling I scared off boys. I took great pride in making high grades, and in retrospect, what young man likes to be upstaged by a smart girl?

Conveniently the TEP house was within a quarter mile of my family's house at Five Points in Athens. So, when we began regular courting, it was easy to study and spend our evenings together, until Dad would arise in his nightgown and shout from the upstairs landing, "Eva, isn't it high time to go to bed?"

Eva and John courting, 1949

My academic program at the University of Georgia was seldom stimulating. The major push seemed to be to make sure I got an "A" in each course. Only a handful of professors left an indelible impression.

One of these was Dr. Nuttycombe, professor of human biology. The students in the huge lecture class of several hundred took notes compulsively on his daily lecture. The course included the most minute details of anatomy and physiology, most of which I have now totally forgotten. But the course had a purpose. In those years, everyone who applied to the University with a high school diploma was admitted. The selection process took place in the freshman year via this human biology course, the level of difficulty sorting out those students who could not succeed in college work. The exceptions, of course, were Charlie Trippi's football stars. No matter what the major, everyone had to take human biology during the first two years of college, and most students dreaded it. One of the beauty queens sat next to me, and I was conscious of her occasional glances at my answer sheet during examination time.

I cannot recall the decisions that directed me to business administration as a major. I did know that I did not want to become a teacher, which was the major career route for the girls. My mother had taken the education courses while I was in high school and complained bitterly about the lack of substance and the amount of busy work. I was vaguely conscious that I would want to work after graduation (planning a career was not yet in vogue). Perhaps I reasoned that business administration would be the best route toward employment.

I suffered through dull personnel management and accounting courses, and must have shown my contempt for one accounting professor who, I felt, was incompetent. As a reward, he gave me a "B" in the course—the only grade below "A" I had ever earned. I was furious, since my test grades led to an "A" in the course, and I appealed the grade. After a second final examination, my grade was changed.

Two courses in business administration were interesting: labor relations and business cycles. The former exposed me, for the first time, to what was happening with labor unions in the nation, and the second one made the dry theory of the economics-principles courses come to life. The labor problems professor, Mr. Segrest, hired me to grade the

EVA GALAMBOS

papers of subsequent classes. The still vivid memory of the depression of the 1930s made the "cycles" course fascinating.

The experience of these two courses, both taught by talented senior faculty, led to my subsequent courses of study: a master's in labor and industrial relations, and a Ph.D. in economics.

By the senior year, when most of the requirements had been met, there was an opportunity to pick upper-level electives in any department. Many of us gravitated to the famed Shakespeare course taught by Professor Roosevelt Walker.

His inspired teaching brought to life the nuances of the Elizabethan language, the connections to British history, and the greater meanings of the tragedies we studied. Unfortunately, there was not enough of this level of instruction.

John's future depended on being admitted to medical school and then on obtaining financing for this endeavor. His grades were fabulous, but returning veterans were flooding the medical school with applications.

The Michael family, who had befriended my parents when we arrived in Athens, again came to our rescue. Their son, Dr. Max Michael, was already established and personally appealed to Emory University on John's behalf. Whether or not this was the deciding factor we never knew, but we never discounted it. In an effort to touch all bases, John had written to Dr. Albert Einstein, who had been helpful to Jewish students as they reached America. In this instance, however, Dr. Einstein wrote back, "forget it." He even intimated that it was unlikely a Jewish boy would be admitted to a medical school in the South. We kept the letter all these years and donated it to the University of Georgia Archives in 1997.

Then came the issue of how he would pay for medical school. Letters and applications went out in all directions, and eventually he got an Emory University Medical School scholarship and a loan from B'nai B'rith, a Jewish organization. During the early years of John's employment, we paid back the loan, and hoped it would help someone else next in line.

By the time John and I graduated together in June 1948 we were strongly committed, and we had jobs at two different summer camps. I was returning to Lake Tiorati, in Harriman Park, New York, where I had been for the past two summers, and he had a post at a nearby camp in New Jersey. Neither of us had a car, of course, and the camps were separated by a mountain range and there was no public transportation available. It took ingenuity to concoct transportation across the mountains so that we could meet on our days off. I recall negotiating with the milk man and the mailman to get rides across the barrier, while John made similar arrangements. Once we ended up hiking on the Appalachian Trail and that hike set the pattern for our pleasure in hiking trails in future years.

The end of the summer of 1948 was bittersweet as we spent a few days together in New York City before parting. I was headed to Urbana, Illinois, to the University of Illinois, where I had a fellowship to study for a master's in labor and industrial relations, and John was returning to Georgia to begin medical school at Emory University. My plan was to finish the master's in one year, so I could get a job, and then to return to Georgia to marry John and work while he attended medical school.

As I look back now, the decision to go to the University of Illinois for a degree in labor was wrong. I was suited for law-school studies, but would not consider them, it, since it would mean staying in Athens, and becoming a student in the law school where my father taught.

The year at Urbana started slowly and ended quickly. At first I was miserable in my separation from John and suffered terribly from hay fever. I never experienced this allergy again. (In retrospect, I think it was probably psychosomatic.) Before long, however, I met a lot of nice young people and lived a crowded academic and social life.

I lived in a rooming house a few blocks from campus. I came prepared to brave the snow and cold, which was so different from Georgia. I had bought a mouton coat. This unsheared lamb fur, which was labeled "mouton," instead of "mutton," for fashion's sake, was almost as wide as long. My rabbit fur-lined boots kept my feet dry, and I was equipped to meet the elements. Most students walked to their classes and engagements. We gathered for meals at the Illini Building, which had remarkably good and cheap institutional food. With all the walking, I shed most of the teenage fat.

The twenty-five to thirty graduate students at the newly formed Institute of Labor and Industrial Relations were a close-knit group, and the faculty was open and interesting. Many were fresh from their experience on the War Labor Board and the actual development of industrial relations in the United States. Professor McPherson, my advisor, had recently served in Japan to help establish labor unions there under General McArthur.

I was determined to write my master's thesis during the nine months of the fellowship, although my advisor felt this was probably not doable. I chose a library topic, rather than a fieldwork subject, because I felt that I could control the pace of library research rather than depending on some outside possibilities for field research.

Dr. Milton Derber taught the social science research course, and it included field research. I recall having to design a survey on some front-burner issue of the day, choosing a sample and then going door-to-door to conduct the interviews. This course, in retrospect, was one of the most useful of my entire year.

I particularly enjoyed the labor-law course offered in the law school, with the exposure that it gave me to the case method and the reasoning process of precedents as the law was interpreted over time. This was a particularly interesting period in labor law, as unions and collective bargaining were becoming more accepted on the American industrial scene.

The most troublesome aspect of completing the master's program was the required internship, which was supposed to give all of us an exposure to the industrial scene and the relations between labor and management. I was determined to return to Atlanta at the end of the spring semester, so that an internship would have to be found in some Atlanta plant, where unions were still almost nonexistent. The Institute was not too happy that I would be fulfilling the requirement in a non-union plant, but finally agreed.

Permanent employment, of course, was much on my mind, as John and I moved toward definite marriage plans. How could I use my degree in labor and industrial relations in Atlanta? The most likely jobs in my field were in the federal government in the Deptartment of Labor, or in the labor relations agencies. While in Illinois, I took the civil service exams, which in those days had many of the characteristics of an IQ test. The reasoning, vocabulary, and mathematics sections were no problem, but I was actually physically uncomfortable when I reached the part of the exam that showed three-dimensional cubes that were rotated throughout the relevant questions. I have no three-dimensional ability of any kind, and I feel sure I did a terrible job on that portion of the test.

On my return to Georgia in the spring of 1949, I was searching for an internship job and filing applications everywhere for subsequent permanent employment. We set our wedding date for October. Veterans had preference for government jobs in those days, and women were still an exception in professional-level jobs.

Uncle Walter, who lived in Atlanta and had many contacts, helped with the internship. I lived with Uncle Walter that summer and ended up at Lovable Brassiere Company, a major manufacturer of a zillion styles of bras. Most of the women on the production line did piece work, and I was assigned to do menial jobs between production steps. For example, I inserted stays into the strapless models, or I cut threads as a bra came off the machine, so the piece-worker would not be slowed down with this unskilled labor.

In the early mornings, in the last breaths of cool air before the stifling heat of summer resumed, I caught the Virginia-Highlands bus and transferred downtown to reach the plant on another bus line. For eight hours each day this boring work went on, and the conversations with a floor of semi-literate women was not exactly rewarding. I would occasionally try to discover from them whether they had any interest in unions, only to find out they had none. The closest I ever came to eliciting any positive response about unions concerned husbands who worked on railroads. They were unionized, and the wives were aware of the benefits. My employer, the Garsons, the Jewish family who owned

Lovable Brassiere Company, would not have been too pleased had they known I was even mentioning the word "union."

As the summer dragged on, with the only good parts being the evenings with John, I continued to earn the minimum seventy-five cents an hour, until for some reason I was asked whether I would like to move to the office. What a relief that was! There I was assigned to write letters to buyers extolling the wonders of the various bra models and their features. I was even allowed to add my own adjectives. The major problem was the heat. There was no air conditioning, even in the office, so the sweat of my hands had a tendency to stain the letters. There was no liquid eraser in those days, either. You had to be correct to begin with or risk ending up with either a mess or a lot of scrap paper.

John and I were married on a Saturday morning in October in the Athens synagogue. John must have been nervous; he left his medical school notes on the Greyhound bus he took to Athens, and we spent the afternoon before the ceremony trying to retrieve the notes. Pre-nuptial headquarters were at my parents' house, and John complains to this day that by the time it was his turn to shower before the wedding, there was no more hot water.

We had a nice dinner for the family at the Holman Hotel. Since Athens was dry in those days, Uncle Walter had brought over the liquid refreshments from Atlanta. This meant nothing to me, since I could count on one hand the number of times I had tasted alcohol by that time. (This included one time on a double date with Tobae Claire Love in Columbia, South Carolina, when I had to ask for the car to be stopped, so I could upchuck the effects of visiting two bars.) After the dinner, John and I loaded our wedding presents in Uncle Walter's car trunk and rode back to Atlanta with him. He delivered us to our apartment on Angier Avenue.

Eva as a reporter with the Locomotive Engineer. She got special permission from the railroad to ride in the locomotive and interview the gentleman on the way to Greenville, S.C.

Putting John Through Medical School

I had been interviewing for jobs here and yonder and generally finding closed doors until I met Joseph Jacobs, a labor lawyer. He came up with the idea that the local weekly labor newspaper could use an editor and introduced me to Cicero Kendrick, the publisher who owned the paper.

This became my first job—associate editor of the *Atlanta Journal of Labor*. What a job title, and what an experience! Mr. Kendrick, with an eighth-grade education, had been a typographical worker, a position which, in those days, offered an opportunity to become fairly literate. He had served in the Georgia General Assembly as one of the three Fulton County representatives at a time when the county unit system only allowed the most populous county three seats, while a county with a hundredth of the population had one seat. The other strange arrangement in those days was the general understanding that labor unions would control one of the three seats. At the time I came to work, Mr. Kendrick had already been replaced by a different labor man, someone he hated.

The newspaper office was on the sixth floor of the Peters Building, next to what is now Underground Atlanta. We had two rooms and an anteroom. Mr. Kendrick occupied one room, and I worked out of the anteroom. My equipment consisted of a typewriter, scissors, and a fan. There was no air conditioning. Another occupant of the floor was a nice young Jewish dentist who was just beginning his practice. When he expected a patient, he would ask me to come into the waiting room to make it appear full.

I was married only one month after starting this job, and the Friday before the wedding as I left, I said to the rest of the staff: "Monday morning I'll be Mrs. Galambos." They tried it and sputtered all kinds of permutations. "It sounds like 'Columbus,'" I coached.

When I came in the next Monday, they said: "Good morning, Mrs. Christopher."

The staff consisted of Mr. Kendrick, two other gentlemen, and me. One of these men was a retired streetcar conductor. His task was as errand boy. He was sent hither and yonder to collect advertising copy, and, as I gradually learned, to pick up outstanding checks so the printer could be paid to put out another edition.

The second man seemed to make phone calls occasionally to procure ads, the lifeline of the paper. I don't recall what his background might have been. His most definite task, however, was to visit the bookie in the back of the Kimball House (an old hotel in the vicinity), and to place bets on the horse races. Then later in the afternoon he would be dispatched there again to collect any winnings.

The copy in the paper, when I arrived, was almost totally canned. My job was to write local copy that would interest the union members who automatically received the paper. Mr. Kendrick made the rounds of the union halls with me and introduced me to the various union leaders. One of my beats was the Georgia General Assembly, one of his old haunts. This was both a revelation and a mystery. There were no copies of the bills being considered. Only a few privileged leaders seemed to have them, and it was impossible to know what the day's agenda might be. There were spittoons all over the place, and the tobacco chewers used theirs regularly. The speaker at that time was a gentleman with a red wig. When he became particularly excited, he would pull off the red wig.

Gradually I filled the weekly with news stories, attempting always to inject as many names of individuals as possible. I remembered from my days with the high school paper how much people like to see their names, or their friends' names, in print. These stories required a lot of legwork and time. I would round out each issue with a feature story about some topic of general interest, and I was even allowed to write the editorials. My freedom in producing the paper was unbelievable. On Fridays, Mr. Kendrick and I would go to Williams Printing Company to lay out the paper. The type would be fitted into the plates, and we would compose headlines to fit the available space. Everything but the linotype composition of the printed columns was done by hand.

Mr. Kendrick introduced me as a new writer to the renowned editor of the Atlanta Constitution—Ralph McGill. His advice has stuck with me all my life: "When you write, try to create pictures with your words." Good advice. Certainly easier said than done.

Soon I met Carolyn Carter, a feature writer for the *Atlanta Journal* weekend magazine. I was a strange phenomenon in those days—a female professional working on a labor paper. She used my experience in a feature about women in new roles that *Mademoiselle* magazine published. One of the best assignments I arranged, with Mr. Kendrick's help, was a feature about a locomotive engineer's life. Somehow we got permission from Southern Railway to break the rule against women in the locomotive, and I traveled the mainline from Atlanta to Greenville, where I spent the night and returned the next day with the same engineer, Mr. Elrod. Shouting to each other over the noise of the engine, I interviewed him, and we got into such a serious conversation that he overlooked a stop in Lula, Ga. Apparently a passenger was waiting to be picked up there, and we had to wait at another stop while a cab brought the stranded lady to the train. This was a great embarrassment to me, since I felt responsible for the mistake that would appear on the engineer's record. The pictures Carolyn Carter took of me reaching up the high step to the locomotive are still impressive to my grandchildren, who wish they could have the same experience. I was wearing a polka dot blue dress and the engineer's cap.

The rent-controlled apartment that John and I found when we married was near Georgia Baptist Hospital on Angier Avenue. This was not a nice part of town even then, but there were few apartments available at the time, and the new ones were above our means. I was earning fifty dollars a week and trying to save a few dollars from that towards future needs. So an apartment with a two-year lease renting at twenty-five dollars a month seemed like a blessing to us, even though we had to buy all the furniture in the place for six hundred dollars. Some of the solid maple bedroom pieces are still in use by one of our children and a friend today. (Other pieces of this set, unfortunately, are no longer desirable because I later decided to paint them purple and orange when I was trying to make one of the bedrooms hip for my teenagers.)

I soon had occasion to get professionally involved in the issue of rent control in Atlanta. Throughout the nation, rents had been controlled during the war. After the war years of no construction, however, housing shortages could raise the rents dramatically, and municipalities were given the option of removing the rent controls. The real estate interests, as might be expected, were most unhappy with the rent controls, and mounted an effort to rescind them. Atlanta Mayor William Hartsfield stood in opposition as he sought to have the city council maintain the controls. The unions were interested in keeping the controls, too, to protect their members.

Mr. Kendrick suggested I help with the campaign to keep the controls. I was fresh from an experience in social science research at the University of Illinois and felt we needed statistics, not just posturing. With the help of Margaret Via, an artist whose husband was engaged in some liberal cause in Atlanta, we designed huge charts to substantiate our argument on housing shortages that merited continued rent controls. The city council and the real-estate representatives were taken by surprise. A union lady (wearing a hat and white gloves, as was the fashionable attire in public at that time) talking statistics, with exhibits—this was most unexpected. I still have the note that Mayor Hartsfield passed to me after the presentation and the subsequent favorable vote, thanking me for the help. I was hooked. I've loved advocacy in front of an audience ever since.

The variety and opportunity for self-initiative in that job were wonderful, and I would have stayed on had it not been for the uncertainty of getting paid. Gradually I became aware of the fact that Mr. Kendrick would appear in the late afternoon soused to the gills.

He would disappear into his office and close the door. (A bottle was hidden there.) The efforts to collect payments for ads so I could be paid on Fridays became more and more frenetic. The most amazing thing I learned was that the stack of unopened mail on his desk grew and grew and apparently included notices from IRS. Social security was a recent innovation in those days, and the social security contributions were not being submitted on my pay. Mysterious collectors would appear and closet themselves with the publisher, and it became obvious that financial affairs were in total disarray. The most amazing spectacle occurred every morning when the mailman appeared. Mr. Kendrick would hold the envelopes up to the light, and if it appeared a check was included, the letter would be opened. If not, it went onto the growing stack. I got so upset about the whole mess that one day I took the bottle and dropped it out of the window of the Peters Building down to the railroad gulch. (This was before the area next to Underground was covered by a plaza.) Before long I collected my last check and left for good.

The rent-controlled apartment on Angier Avenue was on the ground floor of a thirty-year old, two-story building. It was dingy, with no yard or greenery. It was our first nest, however, and it did not really matter to John and me at the time. Our little apartment had a bedroom, living room, tiny kitchen, bath, and an eating corner at the end of the hall. More evenings than not the place was decorated with starched white pants on metal stretchers. John wore white to Grady Hospital every day. They had to be washed and starched before stretching. Finally, came the ironing. For three years, life was measured between the dreaded pants-laundering sessions.

We did try to improve the decor. The kitchen floor was in dismal shape, and we splurged on new red linoleum. John insisted on measuring every tiny twist and turn of the hall and kitchen floor to be covered. Then he drew the design on the reverse side. To his great dismay, when he turned the linoleum right side up, it did not fit at all. Every notch and turn was opposite where it was meant to go. We patched and made do.

Mother contributed to the interior decorating by buying a rug for the living room. Athens had a factory where you could take old clothes and rags and have them reprocessed into rugs at low prices. When the rug went down, as a further embellishment, I decided the hardwood floor was too old and worn around the borders. So I bought shiny black paint and painted the entire border around the rug. When we moved, and took up the rug, the room looked especially sad with its black border.

Crowded as it was, we did have the piano from Athens in the apartment, the piano I had played for so many years. On lonely Saturdays when John worked, I would play the piano and even vocalize by practicing the scales. With the windows open, the kids on the play lots all around would mimic my scales in hilarious amusement.

A mom and pop grocery store occupied the ground space across the street from our apartment, and the customers would park in an open lot on our street. Given the scarcity of off-street parking, the grocery store acquired the lot for its own customers. To prepare the lot for their use, it was enclosed with a chain link fence. We came home from an out-of-town trip with another couple to find our car fenced in, the gate locked.

My cooking left much to be desired, and John wasn't shy about letting me know. The worst episode was stuffed green peppers. I reasoned it would be quicker to cook the hamburger patties separate from the green pepper cases, then combine them and pour tomato soup over all. Little did I know that the Hungarian method was to cook them together, so the flavors would marry. John's comments led to our first big fight.

Another cooking episode was more comical. I was always looking for bargains, and the newspaper office was located close to Broad Street, the main shopping street of the black community. So I would occasionally go and see what bargains were available. The day I brought home a rabbit, which turned out quite tough despite long cooking, coincided with the day John had had to smash a poor rabbit on the head to kill it for an experiment in the laboratory. The last thing he wanted to eat that night was rabbit stew.

My grandmother had lived with us in Athens for several years, but eventually moved to Atlanta to be closer to her son, my uncle Walter Lewy. In Atlanta she had her own small home, and in order to stretch her income, she rented out one of the rooms. She had a remarkable ability to adapt herself—with a smile and warmth that was palpable—to whatever circumstances confronted her. Predictably, Grandmother usually formed close friendships with her renters.

Grandmother loved to host Uncle Walter and family, as well as John and me, for Sunday night dinners. This was the highlight of her week. Well into her seventies, she trudged the several blocks to and from the store with a string handbag to bring home groceries for the delicious dinners she made. After dinner we would all sit together around her radio and laugh together as we listened to "The Henry Aldrich Show."

As young marrieds, our socializing, when John wasn't on call or totally worn out from duties at Grady Hospital, was largely with other medical students and their wives. Among the wives, I was the pariah. My working for a labor newspaper in Atlanta seemed almost like being a communist to some of the wives who had been raised as sheltered clinging vines in Atlanta society or small towns. I was definitely a liberal in those days and ate up the theory that the depression had been caused by lack of purchasing power and that redistribution of wealth had to be good for the economy.

We did manage to have fun on John's days off. The Atlanta Symphony, conducted by Henry Sopkin, played at the municipal auditorium. The auditorium was also used for animal shows and circuses, so you never knew how it would smell. Movies were a welcome and cheap entertainment. We never ate out, but neither did anyone else.

At first we did not have a car. Transportation for our delayed honeymoon to Myrtle Beach that spring was Greyhound bus. After our first year of marriage, we bought Uncle Walter's Ford. The radiator tended to leak. Trips to Blowing Rock, where my parents summered, were never a sure thing. It depended on whether the car wouldn't overheat. Fortunately, there would be creeks and rivers where we could refill the water can we had handy.

One of our early excursions once we had a car was to visit Lake Alatoona, which was just being formed north of Atlanta as a Corps of Engineers project. We anticipated a nice cool swim on a hot summer day. It was quite a letdown to wade into a squishy mud bottom, corn stalks cutting our feet, into water not yet quite deep enough for swimming.

A series of jobs followed my one-year experience at the *Journal of Labor.* First I went to the Georgia State Merit System. In 1950, it had just been granted jurisdiction over a good many state departments that heretofore had been total "political spoils" appointments. Bringing thousands of positions under the merit system called for the development of tests so that the most qualified would be chosen for openings. That led to my designing the first test for clerical workers in Georgia. Besides a typing and dictation test, it entailed a multiple-choice quiz to test reasoning and reading comprehension.

I knew that we needed to apply statistical analysis to determine which individual questions on the proposed test distinguished the best and worst candidates. This is what we call "item analysis." In the days before computers, the only way we could do this was to punch the answers on cards. Then we would put needles through the perforated holes for any one question, and up came the cards with the right answers. The ones that did not come up were the wrong answers. This was called the McBee card system. Before the existence of McBee cards, the analysts would have required examination of each respondent, question by question, all by hand.

By 1951 the country was engaged in the Korean War, and price and wage explosion was again a danger. So Congress established price and wage stabilization boards, with regional sub-boards. Every employer who proposed a wage increase had to petition for approval to the appropriate board. My training was ideal for this, and I bagged a job in the Atlanta regional office.

The petitions were evaluated against a set of criteria that the staff applied. Then the case went before the Board. The two most memorable cases that came across my desk involved McDonnell Douglas in St. Louis and Marineland in Florida. The aircraft-manufacturer case involved thousands of employees and a great deal of lobbying by both employer and labor who wanted the approval so they wouldn't lose their employees in a tight labor market. My role was primarily one of justifying the increases to fit the criteria. The Marineland petition was interesting, meanwhile, because there just were no comparison jobs against which to weigh, for instance, a porpoise-trainer's wage rate. The federal job was fun and paid well—5,200 dollars a year, which seemed like a fortune to us. It ended when John graduated from medical school in June 1952 and we moved to St. Louis for his internship. There I went to work for the International Association of Machinists, helping them prepare the petitions to the wage stabilization board. I was transformed from analyst to advocate.

To the Midwest

There were some twenty business agents in the district office, plus the director and his staff. This was a disciplined place, totally unlike the weird goings on at the *Atlanta Journal of Labor*.

Arrival in St. Louis was traumatic. We found a brand-new apartment complex that looked so bright and clean to us after living in the roach-infested old neighborhood in Atlanta. Before long we found out that this overnight, post-war construction, built with all kinds of government grants, was so shoddy you could not insert even a picture hanger in the wall without it going clear through the wall.

John was so gung-ho he volunteered to start early at the hospital, before the formal July-first date. St. Louis was hotter and more humid than Atlanta. The first Sunday there, I sat in our empty apartment house alone waiting for the moving van with our furniture from Atlanta. When it finally arrived, they refused to unload before receiving a certified check. Nobody had warned us before that a certified check was required, and it was Sunday. What to do? I was frantic, and called on the one person in St. Louis I knew—Steve Loeb, who had been a foreign student at the University of Georgia along with John. Somehow he convinced the movers that they would be paid, and the stuff was unloaded. Since there wasn't so much, I had it arranged and cozy by the time John arrived to see the apartment the next night.

I soon learned how to make the place a little cooler: soak a towel in iced water, and run a fan to distribute a little cooler air. At night all the apartment dwellers congregated outdoors, seeking a little relief.

When John was on call on weekends, we would take our Sunday coffee and newspaper to the air-conditioned office of the chief of thoracic surgery.

Barnes Hospital paid John ten dollars a month, but deducted city income tax of five cents. We lived on my pay and on the hospital's cafeteria. Each night, the house-staff's families would march in with their respective husbands, with two trays of food. The husband or father had layers and layers of food on his tray, to feed his family, while the family trays carried one or two small items. The subsidy went with the job.

The camaraderie among the house-staff families was tremendous, and soon we had many good friends. One special friend was Elizabeth Dowda, or Lib, whose husband was a resident at Barnes. I had bought a sewing machine in order to make my own clothes to save money. My first project was a robe. Lib's mother in Atlanta was an accomplished seamstress, and Lib volunteered to help me sew. "Bring your material and the pattern, and I'll help you with the robe," she said.

To shorten the job, I eliminated the pieces that seemed to me to be superfluous. When Lib inspected the pattern, she asked, "Where are the facings?"

"Oh," I answered. "I figured we didn't need those." She threw up her hands in despair, and that was my introduction to sewing and to the idea that I might need to adopt a different approach to the art. I kept on learning and did a lot of sewing in the years after that.

We then moved on to Chicago, where John did his fellowship at the University of Chicago. I was pregnant and continued working. Eager to avoid miscarriage, which I had suffered through in St. Louis, I took a job that would demand less. I became secretary to the head of the eye department at the University of Chicago Medical School.

Although I did not know shorthand, I made up for that deficit by composing the letters from notes Dr. Newell would give me, and looking up references for his many publications. "At last I have a secretary who can do a bibliography," he would brag to his colleagues, although he was less pleased with me when I failed to recognize a "Queen Anne" table in a storage facility for use in the department's anteroom. I knew nothing about furniture styles, and he seemed to know a great deal.

One of my duties was to talk to the patients who somehow short-circuited the appointments desk. It was a source of considerable amusement to me when Dr. Newell once complained, "Maybe you could try to sound a little less Southern on the phone." I always suspected he did not want his patients to think he had a black secretary—so much for the liberal University of Chicago. At the time there was one black student in the medical school, and he was related to some African potentate.

My first recollection of any personal connection to politics dates to my freshman year at the University of Georgia when President Roosevelt died. As is so often true for many of us regarding when major historical events occurred, I can recall what I was doing when President Roosevelt died. I learned of the news while at the sorority house and then rode my bike for hours as I tried to assimilate the thought that our beloved leader was no more.

During the years following that event, my interest in politics increased dramatically. As a liberal, my choice of labor and industrial relations for the master's program made perfect sense. If one wanted to "reform," one was associated with the movement to even the scales between labor and management through unions. Thus John and I supported Democrats for office in our early years. My first exposure to a national campaign occurred in 1948 when President Truman ran for reelection. I joined other students from the University of Illinois who trekked to some tiny burg out in the prairie waiting for Truman's train to come through on the whistle-stop tour. Eventually he appeared on the platform of the train, and we cheered wildly as he gave his stump campaign speech. Then we joined the local campaign committee, distributing flyers door-to-door in support of the Democrats.

My next memory of a campaign dates to the Adlai Stevenson campaign in 1952. John was then doing his internship in St. Louis, at the hospital for thirty-six hours at a time, then off eight hours before the next round began again. Yet somehow we made time to attend a rally for Adlai Stevenson. We sat in the rafters of a huge convention hall and clapped wildly at Stevenson's cerebral and witty comments in the race he lost to Eisenhower. It was inconceivable to us at the time that the population would fail to recognize Stevenson's superior intellect. Little did we recognize in those days that intellect was not the only attribute necessary for leading the country.

John and I followed national events avidly. We saved our pennies and postponed buying a television set long after most young couples had one, but decided in the spring of 1954 we had to buy one during the Army-McCarthy hearings. This was pure drama, and I devoured each transmission as though it were an installment of a thriller.

We were then living in Chicago, and I was near term with our first baby. On the night of June 3rd, 1954, we were attending a ballet performance in downtown Chicago. A policeman noted my very advanced pregnancy and, after accepting a few dollars, moved a barrier and created a convenient parking spot. This was most fortunate: my water broke during the performance.

As we rushed home to pick up my packed suitcase, it was important to gather up the unread pages of the *Chicago Tribune*, which carried the transcripts of the previous day's Army-McCarthy hearings. Our baby was not born for many hours after we checked into the hospital, and I spent the time devouring the accounts, unwilling to lose out on any juicy bits.

We moved three times during our two years in Chicago, in quest of better apartments near the University of Chicago. Our first apartment was a daylight basement. I always found it kind of disconcerting to lie in bed with John and see only the lower part of legs walking by our windows.

This apartment was near 57th Street. The rent seemed quite reasonable, and after the first heavy rains, we learned why. There was a pipe in the floor that rose upright and was always in the way of furniture. We paid little heed to its purpose, which became clear after a heavy rain. The floodwaters receded down this pipe when too much water leaked in. That led to our first move.

The next apartment was a third floor walk-up, with a bedroom, living room, and cooking alcove. The management painted the apartment before we moved in, and, surprisingly, agreed to our request for a bright red entrance hall. This place was okay until Tobae was born. Her crib was in the bedroom with us, and the cooking alcove served for meal preparation as well as for what seemed to be the constant sterilization of milk bottles. In the 1950s this was required, and filled the entire apartment with steam, as a result of boiling the requisite minutes to sterilize the bottles. The bottle routine took the place of the starch-and-press-the-white-trousers job, which, fortunately, after medical school, was shifted to the hospitals. In the summer, without air-conditioning, the humidity added to the discomfort.

The entire sterilization effort is the more unusual of my recurring nightmares. It alternates with the one about being unprepared for a college test. In the latter, I realize the final is coming up in a mathematics course, and I have not looked at the book all quarter. Of course, however, I was never really in that situation, unlike having to sterilize baby bottles.

The crime rate on the street of the second apartment was extremely high, and we were warned not to leave anything in an unlocked area. So the baby carriage had to be lugged up three flights of stairs every night. Off-street parking did not exist, and, therefore, parking along the curb was a rat race, with never enough space for all the apartment dwellers. One day I came out to find my car with four flat tires. I complained to the police who advised me, "Lady, your car is blocking part of the pedestrian lane. Next time we'll tow it."

Mother came to visit and help me after Tobae was born, and she immediately felt the apartment would not do. By then, I had realized that we were rapidly becoming the minority race in the building, which, coming from the South, was an unusual situation for me. So we put our name on the university housing list for a bigger place, and a few months later moved to Maryland Avenue, just one block from the Midway.

Now we had a huge apartment, with empty rooms strung with laundry lines to dry the diapers. It was also a third-floor walk-up, and the shape of the apartments led to the moniker of "Pullman apartment":

a string of rooms off a long, narrow hall. Only the front and the back room had windows, the rest being wall-locked. So, Tobae got the front room with a window, and we took the back room for our bedroom. The distance in between made it difficult to hear her cry, but she was such a happy baby that we often found her playing and talking to her toys in the crib long before she'd fuss.

The university was generous and painted the apartment before we moved into it. We chose chartreuse and watermelon pink for two of the windowless rooms. We had plenty of space for socializing, and one night even had a dance in those rooms. We hung the laundry in one of the unused rooms. The washing machine, a recent acquisition, was in the basement of the apartment house.

An Indian family lived on the floor below us, and the smell of their cooking left an indelible dislike of anything curried in John's taste buds. There was also constant Indian music, which eventually lost its charm.

John was working with the two foremost experts in ulcerative colitis, and the disease and associated research were much discussed in our conversations. Eventually John came home with an Italian research article about ulcerative colitis that someone wanted translated. I worked on it laboriously, one word at a time. At the end we pretty well had the body of the article, but were somewhat uncertain whether or not the hypothesis was proven or disproved. Anyway, we were paid twenty dollars to translate the article, and nobody ever complained that we came up with the wrong ending. We used the money to buy a slide projector. (This was an old-fashioned one, into which one inserted a slide at a time.) We did not keep it long enough for it to attain antique value.

One unwelcome outcome of the ulcerative-colitis research was that I came down with the symptoms. I would be afraid to take Tobae on her daily outing to the Midway at the University of Chicago because I might need to hightail it to the bathroom. Since I was pregnant, it was somewhat disquieting that I was losing instead of gaining weight.

Before long the head of the gastro-intestinal department, Dr. Walter

Palmer, examined me. He was a wonderfully kind doctor, famous for his bedside manner. The house staff always marveled at Dr. Palmer's technique of backing out of the patient's hospital room, seeming to give the patient his total, undivided sympathy and attention, while he was already on the way to the next room, surrounded by the adoring house staff.

My most vivid memory of the Palmer visit entails walking down the hall from one examining room to another carrying my corset. In order to protect my back, which often hurt from carrying Tobae up three flights of stairs, the obstetrician had prescribed an old-fashioned corset, complete with stays, that fastened with a multitude of strings.

I was terribly embarrassed to be carrying this apparatus around between examinations. In the end, my malady was purely imagined. The symptoms were psychosomatic, and probably due to our worries about John's impending service in the Korean War—and translating that article.

He had received induction papers to serve as a doctor in the Korean War. Somehow after complicated correspondence and repeated visits to the recruiting office, his assignment was changed to the Public Health Service, to be stationed in Atlanta, Georgia.

We would be going home to have our second child, and, we hoped, to settle down. I was more than ready.

Neighbors, Houses, and Rabble-Rousing Ladies

In the spring of 1955, John came to Atlanta and over one weekend, with the help of Uncle Walter, he bought our first house on McJenkin Drive in DeKalb County. I bugged him when he returned to Chicago, "Draw me a house plan. Where is the kitchen? What kind of windows?" He was a little vague. But in a few weeks the packers arrived for our move to Atlanta. This was our one and only move that packers handled, since the Public Health Service was paying for it. When we unpacked in Atlanta, we found that even some empty cereal boxes had been packed.

I was six months pregnant, so John drove our car to Atlanta and I enjoyed my first airplane ride, with Tobae and a teddy bear that was almost the same size as she was. I was ecstatic about our new home—a brand new brick bungalow.

It seemed like heaven—a yard, woods in the back, two bedrooms and a den, and a sparkling tiled bathroom. The full basement afforded storage and play space for active little children. Johnny was born three months after we moved in, in September 1955, so we had two babies fifteen months apart. He cried a great deal more than Tobae had as a newborn, and in retrospect, probably suffered from colic.

When Johnny was only a few months old, I found a strange lump, about the size of a pecan, just above my right knee. Everyone was grim faced as Mother came to stay with the two babies, and I was hospitalized. "Why is the house staff so fascinated with my leg?" I inquired as a myriad of specialists poked and examined. The lump was removed, and the frozen sections analyzed, and to John's great relief, it was some pseudo-malignancy with a long name that had developed from the repeated stress on my leg as I rocked the baby carriage. My hands were usually engaged in some household task or occupying the one-year old, so my leg, just above the right knee, did the rocking.

The neighbor on the left side, Dot Malone, soon became friendly. She had two children and the older one was only slightly older than Tobae. It was natural that we would become friends and that our children would play together. Eventually they all had some kind of riding toy (trikes, police cars, etc.) and in the cool of the summer evenings, we would sit at the curb and watch the little ones riding up and down in great glee.

But the family on the left side never called. In those days, established neighbors called on new ones, and yet she never darkened the doorway. Many years later Dot Malone confided that the Breitenbachs were dismayed that a Jewish family had moved next to their house. This is one of the few overt incidents of anti-Semitism I ever experienced in Atlanta. The other event happened when Tobae attended Girl Scout camp at Red Top Mountain, north of Lake Allatoona. One of her bunkmates made her stay miserable with taunts about Tobae's religion, and the mother, who was a counselor at the camp, condoned the taunting. I did complain about this, after I learned of it, to the Girl Scout headquarters. Nothing hurts one so bad as when one's child is hurt. As to our neighbors, a lovely, elderly couple with whom we became friends soon replaced the unfriendly family.

Outdoor activity and gardening beckoned from the very beginning of life at McJenkin Drive. We planted a magnolia in the front in 1955, which is now a huge, stately specimen. Our *Etoile de Holland* climbing rose in the back of the house was a mass of red blossoms after the first two seasons. In the front, we had spring and summer flowers, and John even experimented with redwood tree seedlings, which were doomed to die in the hot South. Gardening was soon irrevocably in our blood.

As John's income improved, we hired household help. With each child's birth, I graduated to one more day of help, so that by the time Michael was born in 1958, I had a maid three days a week.

The procession of different maids seemed endless. They would work a while and then quit. Finally I found elderly Annie Ruth, who lacked one eye. She never explained how that had happened. In the hot days of July 1958 as I was wishing the next baby would hurry up and be born, she counseled, "Ms. Eva, you'd better get ya some of them eggplant. That'll bring it on." Annie Ruth was right on target. Michael was born twenty-four hours later.

Annie Ruth was quite faithful for two years, until we went to the beach. "Annie Ruth," I asked, "would you like to go to Florida with us for a week and look after Michael while we're there?"

"Yes'm, yes'm, I'd shore love to go." she replied. She'd never been further than a few miles out of Atlanta and indicated that she felt that her husband could do without her for a week. She seemed to look forward to fishing in the surf in Florida.

It turned out to be a nightmare. John and I had not anticipated the problems she might encounter at restaurants or filling stations as we drove south. She refused to let us inquire whether she would be welcome in a place, probably in fear she would be rejected. She made do with what we brought out for her to eat, and I don't remember now how we solved the bathroom problem. At any rate, during the week at the beach at Long Boat Key, where she did look after Michael, she became increasingly homesick. After her return to Atlanta, I never saw her again. She did not call or tell me why, but we figured it out. The trip through the tightly segregated South was a terrible mistake, and we should never have asked her to go.

After experimenting with a series of maids who would come maybe once or twice, I finally found Myrtle, who was as wide as she was tall. It seemed impossible to me that she would have the agility to clean and to pick up the baby, but she did both admirably for several years. The children were very fond of Myrtle. Unfortunately, health problems eventually made her unable to work.

Then came Rebie, a slight black lady who had just had her third baby and desperately wanted work. Her grandmother would look after the baby. I would try to help Rebie, meanwhile, by passing on the outgrown clothes for her children. We all loved Rebie, especially the way she answered the phone. She'd pick it up and immediately say, "two fy-fy, fow, fow three ow." Rebie had a fourth child eventually, but worked until the very end, and soon came back. Her loyalty was amazing, but she started to miss more and more days. Occasionally she would appear with a split lip, or a bruised face. "My husband done hit me," she would explain. I tried to counsel her and offer suggestions about how to leave him.

The missed days became more frequent, with more and more tales of woe. Eventually, the lady who employed Rebie on the two days I did not have her called. "Eva," she exclaimed excitedly. "I just want to tell you why Rebie is not at your house today. I was called down to the police and had to bail her out. She'd been caught making a scene after drinking too much and the police locked her up." I could not believe it. Rebie was not the victim of her husband's excesses, but of her own. This had been going on under my nose, and I had missed it.

The mailman came to the door soon thereafter. "Where is Rebie?" he asked. I explained what had happened, and he noted, "Yep, I'd been smelling it on her breath through the last few months. Didn't you know she was nipping while at your house?"

At that point, it registered with John that the level in his liquor bottles seemed to have been declining mysteriously. I had been so concerned about whether she would continue to come, and so dreading the process of looking for another maid that I had failed to see what was happening.

All through those early years with the small children, I did as much cleaning alone as possible, so that when the maid arrived, I could be out the door. I yearned for intellectual contact and grownups.

Often my destination was some meeting of the League of Women Voters, to which I gravitated in an effort to be involved in current affairs. My inclination was still to believe in government solutions, and I saw little wrong with centralization of power and control. I thought the world was rational and could be planned from the top on down. From this perspective, it made no sense to me in those days that the Atlanta area was composed of a multiplicity of governmental units, all doing their own thing. I collected the data, and edited a League of Women Voters publication, "Atlanta—50 Governments!" which was well received in the community.

While I was active in the DeKalb County League of Women Voters, I recognized that Eleanor Richardson was a woman of unusual talents. I nominated her for president of the DeKalb League, after having to call her husband to talk him into it. She rose rapidly from that spot to head the Georgia League and eventually became a member of the Georgia House of Representatives. I had not seen Eleanor for many years and was pleasantly surprised when she and her husband turned out to be the owners of the beautiful sailboat docked on the slip opposite ours.

With Tobae and Johnny in school, Michael often accompanied me to meetings of the League of Women Voters. We would take along his box of soldiers or toy cars. He played contentedly under the conference table. Occasionally, he would search for my legs so he could surface for a trip to the bathroom. He was a happy, easy child. The grown-ups loved him.

My other excursion to the outside world while the children were toddlers was to join the Auxiliary to the Atlanta Medical Association. I felt that it would help John's career if I joined the ladies and became part of the group. John's growing renown as a liver expert soon made it clear that his standing certainly did not depend on my socializing with the ladies.

I joined the lunches and attended the fashion shows and talks on gardening. It wasn't long before I became astounded by how shallow the whole thing was. We were living in a time when the daily local news centered on whether our state would close all the public schools rather than integrate them under federal mandates. In Georgia, the politicians were still maintaining that desegregation would happen over their dead bodies. The idea of talking fashions and flower arranging in this context bothered me.

I finally got up the nerve to discuss with one of the younger ladies in a leadership position, Mrs. Midge Lee, whether we could put on a program on the issue of closing the schools. Enough of the leadership agreed—amazingly, I thought—and a panel was assembled to discuss the issue. The topic caused quite a stir, and, of course, both sides were represented: close the schools, and keep them open and integrate.

A decade later I had occasion to think back on that episode. I was beginning my career as an economic consultant, and one of the first assignments that fell in my lap was to design a survey on how to peacefully integrate the teaching staffs of the public schools in Atlanta. Much of this exercise centered on how to soften attitudes and create a fairly smooth transition. The shuffling of teachers to insure the proper racial ratios affected the high school that my youngsters attended. Unfortunately, the process did not always have a happy result. Tobae's science teacher was one of the transferred minority instructors. Tobae came home one day explaining to her dad that the liver was located in the proximate location of her heart. That raised his eyebrows. Before long, he and two other doctors on the same street offered to augment instruction in the science class. Of course, these sporadic visits probably did little to strengthen the curriculum.

I felt a little guilty in 1959 even broaching the idea of another house to John. We lived in a perfectly adequate one, but I was beginning to feel the lure of more space and more style. The conventional, traditional homes were not to our liking, and John soon agreed, "Go look at lots." That suggestion eventually led us to 5070 Trimble Road, a beautiful two-acre tract, on what was still a gravel road, with water lines just being dug by Fulton County.

For more than a year, we visited the lot and tried to conquer the underbrush. With the children in tow, and Michael often happily playing in a puddle covered from head to toe in mud, we gradually cleared more and more of the lot. A lovely creek flowed through the rear, over which we imagined that we would eventually have a bridge. A huge water oak shaded one side of the backyard and tall pines rose all along the western lot line. In the front we liberated old apple trees that had been planted in what must once have been a pasture. They attracted hundreds of birds, but produced only cooking apples.

In the meantime we drew plans and more plans, with the help of Andre Steiner, a Czechoslovakian architect specializing in the contemporary style. He designed houses after his full-time duties as a planner—eventually the chief planner—with Robert and Company. His ideas were clean and impressive, and produced a beautiful contemporary house designed to fit our family of five, a house which served us well for thirty-two years. The original architectural drawings are in the archives of the Atlanta History Center because they serve as a leading example of the contemporary, flat-roof style in the Atlanta area.

Seeing our redwood house going up in the spring of 1960 was a joy. I spent many hours around the building site trying to clear underbrush. (The old house, luckily, sold quite easily.) In the new house, we had three bedrooms (the boys shared one), a family room, a combined living and dining room, and an initially unfinished lower level. The house was quite unusual compared to the typical ranch style. The ceiling rose from the standard nine-foot level to a soaring fifteen feet at its highest point in the living room. The window wall, with sliding glass doors, led to the patio, lining the entire length of the back of the house. It was a very contemporary split level, with exposed beams and an open floor plan. The siding was redwood, and we covered the wooden front doors with copper sheets, which we weathered with chemicals.

We moved in July 1960, with workmen all around us for many weeks to come. It was heaven to be there. I still dream of life in the house that we occupied for thirty-two happy years. I was heartbroken when I visited the site as the house was being torn down to make room for new houses. Nothing was saved: not any of the redwood siding of the house, not the massive fir beam that had been ordered from California to hold up the flat roof, not even the multi-colored leaded glass in the clerestory windows. The bulldozer operator told me he had seven days to demolish the existing homes, and thus no time to salvage anything of value. The irony was that in their haste the developers somehow ran afoul of stream preservation ordinance and were put on "stop work" orders because of this infraction.

The amount of yard work to be done seemed overwhelming, but somehow, year-by-year the place became a landscaped heaven. The initial front lawn was put in with the help of an old man who lived about a mile from the house in the old Linwood black neighborhood in DeKalb County. He brought a plow and a pair of mules and prepared the front yard. In the years to come it never lost its many bumps and dips, and the featured grass was "natural." Immediately around the house we graded properly and planted individual tufts of zosya grass, which eventually grew into a thick carpet.

Impatiens liked our soil and climate, and by the seventies large areas of the yard were covered by volunteer plants that bloomed their hearts out in the late summer. They produced seedpods in the fall that popped and flung the seeds in many directions. The impatiens spread ever wider in the yard. When we moved to Wing Mill, we brought a large supply of the seeds, but they never took hold here.

In our hurry to civilize our wilderness, we planted ivy sprigs in many areas of the Trimble Road lot. Old Dr. Sellers, whose son also built on Trimble Road, was the source of the ivy. "You'll be sorry," he warned me. "The first year it sleeps, the second year it creeps, and the third year it leaps." I found out what he meant, and one of the most time-consuming jobs in later years was cutting the ivy back and preventing further growth. The rider mower, furthermore, could cut the grass acreage, but the ivy had to be cut by hand.

We put in ivy along the driveway under the hardwood trees, and the home next door, occupied by renters, was eventually covered with ivy to the roof.

Our home on Trimble Road was still surrounded by acres and acres of undeveloped wilderness. As the children grew older, the boys especially roamed through the forests to their secret forts, bridging creeks and swinging on vines. By the time Johnny and Michael were eight and five they had a pellet and bb gun, respectively, and would join John in the woods for target practice. I tagged along for the outings. On one such occasion, I sniffed in the air and remarked, "I smell something fermenting." We investigated and discovered fumes rising from a small hole in the ground. They came from a hidden whiskey still where a full brew of mash was working. On further investigation we came upon a middle-aged, black man hiding behind a tree. When confronted, the man said he was out training his dog to catch rabbits. We said goodbye and kept looking. By following a trail we discovered an automobile with several filled gallon glass jars and other moonshine equipment in the open trunk.

Tobae was told it was her job to memorize the tag number, which was reported to the detectives. The police traced it and arrested the moonshiner. The still's 500-gallon capacity could produce about $14,000 worth of moonshine each week.

The local newspaper picked up the story, and for some reason it was forwarded to the United Press syndicate. The kids had gleefully described the adventure to the reporter and had given me credit for a "super-sensitive nose," a feature that was highlighted in headlines across the country. We had notes from friends in Chicago inquiring about my big sniffer.

Apparently not everyone felt we did the right thing by calling the police. We had anonymous telephone callers, complaining, "Why did you have to mess with that man's business?" The frontier days of "live and let live" were not that far gone.

This was not the end of the episode. The fellow came back and rebuilt his still. This time, before calling the police, John salvaged some of the product, and ran it through his lab to make sure it was not lead poisoned. Assured it was not, we threw a rye whiskey party for the neighbors. All who sampled it indicated it was really quite good. The police eventually caught the moonshiner in the woods when he returned once more. His girlfriend lived nearby, and the creek was conveniently located for his business after visiting his paramour. The police shot him in the leg the third time. He ended up at Grady Hospital, where John saw him on the wards.

The suburban neighborhood in which we lived in the sixties had other interesting aspects. Half a mile up Peachtree Dunwoody Road was a distinctive two-story, stone house occupied by the "numbers queen." This was in the days before a legal lottery existed in Georgia. A subterranean lottery was big business, however, and there were locations downtown where men would disappear at noon to pick their numbers, which were somehow keyed to horse races. The police knew what was going on, but I was never aware of our nearby lottery queen being so much as harassed by them.

Across the street from the numbers queen lived a family that ran a séance parlor. On Friday nights, cars with out-of-county tags from all over north Georgia would park on the narrow shoulders. Their occupants attended sessions that put them in touch with their departed loved ones.

Occasional picnics were another interesting occurrence in the neighborhood. They took place on the right-of-way at the major intersection of Peachtree Dunwoody Road and Windsor Parkway. This was in the days when Fulton County operated a prison camp, using the inmates to clean up the right-of-ways and to pick up trash. They were overseen by a couple of guards. On a pretty day, a card table would emerge from the van, with a tablecloth, and a picnic was spread out for the guards, while the inmates sat on the grass. I had the privilege of partaking of the prison-camp food on one occasion. From some connection with my civic activities, I was invited to lunch at the prison camp, which in those days grew vegetables and raised farm animals to feed the inmates. (One could also arrange for catering by the prison camp if one had sufficient pull with one of the county commissioners.) I was astounded when I was seated in the dining area at the prison camp as the inmates, clad with white gloves, served a huge and delicious meal of homemade vegetables, corn bread, and ribs. It was a much heavier lunch than I was normally accustomed to eating.

One of the amusements we women indulged in as we raised our small children was playing bridge. Week after week, we would have foursomes, which served as much for psychotherapy as for bridge playing. Much of the discussion centered on our frustration in trying to join the working world. I was the only one of the group who had worked professionally before the children were born, but we were all infected with the new message of the feminist movement that to fulfill themselves women had to be "productive" in jobs.

One of the bridge players was Mickey Silverstein, who was particularly frustrated with her search to find a new role. She and I talked at length about the need for a bookstore in Atlanta that would feature paperbacks. At the time, the only place where one could buy these was at the airport concession and other newsstands, which a Mr. Elsas owned.

Mickey and I went so far as to write the publishers of paperbacks to inquire how we could obtain their books to sell locally, and in each case we were referred to their Atlanta dealer—Mr. Elsas. We went to see him, and told him we were interested in opening a store in the northern section of Atlanta to sell paperbacks. "Oh, ladies," Mr. Elsas replied, "There is no demand for those in the area; the venture would never fly." He was not honest enough to tell us he was planning to launch the paperback store in the new Lenox Mall.

John cautioned me about being in business with Mickey. "You'll end up being in the store, and she'll be running around and having interviews." Mickey eventually became a talk show host in Atlanta with another gal who had played bridge. Together they were the first in town to inject spice and sex allusions into radio discussions. Their overly frank talk soon got them into trouble, and they were summoned to the Georgia House of Representatives. Mickey and Teddi had described the Speaker as managing a "stableful of women," and they had to retract their statements. The station fired them.

Mickey was inventive and pursued new entrepreneurial projects. Her next venture involved a survey questionnaire to all her friends. We were invited to answer all kinds of loaded questions about our aspirations, home life, and relationships with our husbands. This "research" provided the gist of her book, *Have You Had It in the Kitchen?* I was naive enough not to comprehend the double entendre of the title until the night of the autograph party. The book included all kinds of modern prescriptions on how to combine housework and fun. For example, after a busy day in the office, the recipe was to buy frozen food, open a bottle of wine, illuminate the dinner table with candles, and serve the meal in a slinky negligee. Mickey soon outgrew Atlanta, and moved to Los Angeles, after a bitter divorce.

It is impossible to forget the bridge game at Esther Rawn's home in November 1963, when the news flashed that President Kennedy had been shot. The game ceased abruptly as we tried to accommodate to what we did not want to believe. In those days, John and I were still Democrats, and total admirers of the Kennedys. As so many other families, we were devastated. The next three days, we all sat in front of the television set transfixed at the replay of events that put our nation into a time of mourning.

Before Mickey left town for greater glories in Los Angeles, I was involved with her in further ventures. At that time, increasing interest centered on the Chattahoochee River. Mickey and I were scouting for desirable investment land and "discovered" the lovely "Island Ford" area between Roswell and Sandy Springs on the Chattahoochee River. We immediately sensed this would make a fabulous park site and proceeded to try to develop the interest of the county commissioners in acquiring the site. Commissioner Jim Aldredge visited our home, and we set up chairs in what was then still an empty and unfurnished living room. We spoke enthusiastically about the beauty of the site and urged that the county acquire it. He listened politely.

Many, many years later this site, along with many others along the shores of the Chattahoochee River were acquired by the federal government for the national-recreation-area parks which now provide John and me with our favorite trails throughout the cooler months. We've explored every trail on the system; we are amazed how underutilized most of them remain even today. That's to our benefit, however.

When Mickey and I were exploring our environs, it was becoming obvious that Atlanta was exploding and that proper land investments would pay off one day. Mickey and I traipsed over tract after tract and settled on acreage next to the Chattahoochee River on Eves Road that was being offered at $440 per acre. We put together a "syndicate," or group of friends, to participate in this venture. Someone suggested that we ought to have a lawyer to advise us and ensure that we weren't doing the wrong thing. Bob Lipshutz was drafted, and he participated in a meeting of the group in our home to discuss the venture.

"You must have it appraised," Bob cautioned. The appraisal came in at four hundred per acre, which was forty less than the listed price. Bob's caution was enough to disband the group. The husbands had harbored their inner doubts about the degree of business sense the two wives who came up with the plan had. The land is now a prime subdivision, with lots selling at $200,000 per acre. Bob Lipshutz ended up going to Washington to dispense legal counsel to President Jimmy Carter.

During this same period in the seventies, land-speculation fever ran high, and we did not escape it. John Young, my good friend Martha's oldest son, had entered the real estate business and was putting together syndicates for purchase of land. The federal government allowed tax benefits for such investments, and Atlanta was looking for another airport site. The city purchased land in Paulding County, which became John Young's special mission. Toward the end of every year, he would appear and suggest it was time for another tax shelter in Paulding County. Twice I fell for it. A management company, involving some ten partners, managed the first syndicate. The second one consisted of us, plus two medical colleagues (Woody Cobbs and John Preedy). The first partnership collapsed when the real estate market dropped, and the Atlanta airport site evaporated. I determined not to lose the second one, too. The three couples involved in the deal kept the payments up, and eventually subdivided the tract into lots, and got out of the investment without losses, having gained the tax shelter in the intervening years. A lot of effort was needed to deal with Paulding County to gain their approval for our subdivision plat. The purchasers of the lots all made down payments, and for years I was collecting monthly checks and keeping accounts on their purchases.

I grew up in a household that was very interested in the politics of the day. Despite limited income, one of mother's small luxuries was the Sunday *New York Times*. So I grew up aware of what was going on nationally and that politics were important. In the 1940s I realized that we were especially grateful to President Roosevelt for his role in fighting Nazi Germany. So it was quite understandable that we were favorably inclined to the politics that came out of that period. Moreover, my father grew up during the time when Germany instituted national social-benefit programs, which he felt were the only modern way of taking care of retired folks. So there was a tilt in the household toward government programs.

My economics education in undergraduate school was not yet Keynesian. In fact it took a while for the philosophy of John Maynard Keynes to permeate into undergraduate curricula. Pump priming by the federal government, however, was much in vogue and permeated the atmosphere of the 1940s as I was becoming politically awake.

It was not until I returned to higher education in the mid-sixties, embarking on the Ph.D. in economics that I was exposed to the more conservative foundation of the discipline. Indeed, I did not read Adam Smith's *The Wealth of Nations,* nor Milton Friedman's *A Time to Choose,* until I began the program. These writers, as well as the Chicago School of Economics, which was then very prominent in the new publications, exposed me to a much firmer understanding of what produces economic growth and to the disincentives to growth that many government programs entail.

A combination of reasons, therefore, led to our gradual conversion from liberals to staunch conservatives. Most basic, perhaps, was the growing realization of the ever-larger proportion of our income that was going toward taxes. It is a truism that young people tend to be more emotional, have little of their own to protect, and are more liberal about sharing and redistributing. Older people, who have more to conserve, become less emotional and less eager to redistribute income. This was especially true in our case.

When we finally had money, it was especially clear because we had been scraping savings together for years. While earning fifty dollars a week at the *Atlanta Journal of Labor,* for example, I was dedicating a portion to savings. We ate potatoes and noodles, and I bought cheap cuts of meat on Broad Street in downtown Atlanta. From job to job, my salary had improved, and I was determined always to squirrel some away. Thus by the time we moved to Atlanta in 1955 for John's start at the Public Health Service, we had just enough for a down payment on the first house, the McJenkin Drive house. John still recalls coming to Atlanta to pick out a house with Uncle Walter. After two days, a decision was made, and a closing took place. That night, in the half-wakeful period before deep sleep, John had a nightmare that he would not be able to meet the payments on the loan he had just taken out. The next morning he went over the arithmetic again, and prospects seemed brighter. After living so frugally for so many years, the ever-increasing bite of income going to taxes slowly transformed our liberal leanings to a more conservative outlook.

The History Class

The "History Class of 1884" served as an intellectual stimulus for me for many years. A group of ladies from New England formed this voluntary association in 1884 to overcome the lack of intellectual life they encountered in Atlanta. A theme is picked for the year, and each of the twenty or so members must prepare a researched paper on a given topic within the theme. The group has survived to the present, and I was thrilled when my good friend Martha Young nominated me for membership in the organization.

Each year I prepared a paper on a topic that typically I knew nothing about. It really forced me to read and understand a period and to gain a great appreciation for reading historical works, which I did not have before. The themes varied widely from year to year. My favorite one, which ran for two successive years, dealt with the major legal trials of mankind. The papers ranged from Pontius Pilate to Sacco Vanzetti. My choice for one of those two years was the Dreyfus case. I suggested to the group that we put together our papers to publish an anthology of the world's famous trials, but I could not gain enough support.

The History Class exposed me to learning much more about geography and history than I ever had before. Mostly the papers from the other members were enjoyable, but I never could remember much from a paper someone else read. I think it was the depth of research for my own own papers that left a lasting impression. The twenty ladies met at the reader's home; absolutely no refreshments were allowed. This practice ran totally counter to the usual Southern hospitality mores, and yet we faithfully adhered to the rules. The group was composed of ladies near my age, but with many different philosophical and political perspectives.

One year, my subject was George Bernard Shaw, and I decided the best way to illustrate his genius was by having the group read parts of a play. I chose *Major Barbara*, and invited my old, mischievous friend Gene to join the members of the class in reading various parts. One of the twins, Sue Brown, became a beauty queen in the university yearbook, somewhere around 1948, and she then enrolled in the law school. Eventually she worked in her father's law office and had quite a career teaching business law in South Carolina. Gene, meanwhile, had married Bob Weldon and lived with him in Griffin. Unbelievably, when it came time to read her lines, she could not read them correctly. Later, after everyone else had departed, she told John and me that she was having trouble with her eyes. She could not see the ends of the lines on a page. Her eye doctor in Griffin had just prescribed new glasses, and they did not help at all.

John performed a few tests on her and on the spot concluded she had a neurological problem, and asked she immediately visit a specialist. This was arranged, and to our great dismay, Gene was diagnosed as having an aneurysm in her brain, which affected her eyesight. The specialist indicated surgery was very problematic.

Gene went on with her life courageously, even completing a scheduled trip to Europe with a friend that same spring. A few weeks after her return from the trip, the aneurysm burst, and she died suddenly. It was a terrible loss to me.

The exposure to history and geography, which became ever more interesting through my years with the History Class led me to a small historical work of my own. I had always been somewhat curious about the origin of street and place names in the Atlanta area. Who were these people whose names were plastered over our maps? What did they do?

What about all the streets named "Ferry"? Where were these ferries and how did they work?

So I decided to do a little research in local libraries and their archives and any other sources I could dig up and produced a slender volume, "What's in a Name?" I had a lot of fun and discovery, and there seemed to be quite a bit of local interest in it among civic and garden clubs of the Atlanta area.

I self-published with a small publishing firm in Georgia. I was totally responsible for the marketing of the booklet, which opened up another whole world to me. Dealing with book distributors to retailers turned out to be a nightmare. The author is at the very bottom of the chain, handing over books to the distributor and then receiving small checks as retailers report sales to the distributor. I reprinted the booklet once, and then decided marketing books was not my game. I turned over the printing rights to the Atlanta History Center since their gift store had been one of my best outlets for sales.

One total delusion about selling the book occurred in connection with the 1996 Olympics in Atlanta. I imagined that visitors to Atlanta would be eager to obtain some light reading about the city and its history, and I got the address of the man to whom Mayor Campbell had given the rights to all the stalls and street vendors for the Olympics.

Naively, it turns out, I assumed he would be interested and visited what I thought would be his office. It turned out to be a box at a UPS mailing station.

Balancing the Garish with Greenery

My first encounter with the Fulton County zoning process occurred while we were still building the Trimble Road house. A zoning sign was posted on our street indicating an effort to subdivide the land into smaller lots. This trip to the downtown courthouse was the beginning of many such expeditions and an exercise in total frustration. In years to come the posting of these signs always raised my blood pressure. "Oh, no," I would think. "Another fight. Another round of calling and persuading neighbors to raise troops to object at endless commission meetings downtown." It gradually became apparent that the county commissioners listened to the neighbors out of politeness, but zoned as they pleased. The developers made contributions to the election of the commissioners, and we residents never had a chance. Yet we fought on and on.

During the 1980s the bribes from petitioners to the commissioners became so blatant that they led to the conviction and jail terms for two of them. The most egregious aspect of the zoning process entailed the votes of several commissioners who have absolutely no constituents within the unincorporated area of Fulton County. They could inflict unwanted development on Sandy Springs with impunity, secure in the knowledge there would never be any *quid pro quo* since zoning in their districts is handled by another jurisdiction.

The recurring distress led to the first effort at organizing the community. Joseph Jacobs and I gathered other interested individuals and formed the Sandy Springs Planning Council. For several years we met monthly to go over the rezoning petitions on the county agenda and formulate positions. Then one of us would appear at the county commission meeting and express the council's position. This did little good, since the membership of the organization was not large enough. The zoning went on and on, including the ugliness of the central commercial strip.

By the mid-sixties I had become involved with the first effort to do something about the horrible Roswell Road. As the central spine of the town, it was experiencing commercial growth, but mostly minimalist construction: cinder blocks, barely disguised, with a proliferation of garish advertising signs. It had no sidewalks. It was a totally negative assault on the senses. One of the memorable signs was for an early fast food outlet called "Chicken in a Basket." A huge basket—into which a chicken was laying an egg—protruded over the right of way.

Gas station requests were also especially prolific in the 1960s. Somehow it seemed to be the oil companies' policy to put one almost at every block. Each station featured a multitude of signs with no aesthetic awareness evident in the design of the structure.

Hope springs eternal, and the community decided to construct a grand design for the heart of Sandy Springs. A few business property owners joined in the effort, most notably Western Electric, the major employment center in Sandy Springs at that time. This company had obtained its commercial zoning after a long and bitter battle with the surrounding residential neighborhood in the early 1960s.

Western Electric was actually the only commercial establishment on Roswell Road with decent landscaping, setbacks, and trees in the parking lot. Later it became Lucent Technologies, still an attractive contrast to most of the commercial blight. Today it is gone, replaced by a very attractive private school and new townhomes.

Any planning exercise invariably entails a lot of meetings to insure community input. The effort in Sandy Springs was no different. Western Electric hosted gathering after gathering, and helped raise the modest sum of $25,000, which was enough to buy a plan in those days. The architectural firm of Roberts and Company was engaged with Andre

Steiner as the leading planner. Andre (who, as mentioned previously, was the architect for our Trimble Road home) had big dreams. A beautiful, but totally unrealistic plan was the final outcome. A copy of it is still available in the Sandy Springs library. It called for elegant plazas and high-rise office-and- commercial development on Roswell Road, with sidewalks to connect the open spaces and public parking garage. Anchoring the central commercial area would be a vertical mall, since land assembly of the many small parcels would negate the usual expanse of horizontal parking associated with malls.

We visited the owners of Rich's Department Store to try to entice them into the new community design, with total failure. They were already planning Perimeter Mall, about two miles distant, where acres and acres of virgin land could be paved over for horizontal development.

Rich's did offer its alternative: "We're going to build a Richway Discount store in the center of Sandy Springs." We were crestfallen. The Richway Discount stores that had already been built elsewhere resembled warehouses, in yellow mustard finish, topped by garish, bright green and red buttresses on top of the roof. We were aghast.

I remember visiting Joel Goldberg, then CEO of Rich's, in his downtown office.

"Please, Mr. Goldberg, don't inflict that monstrosity on the center of Sandy Springs."

"Why, it's beautiful," he countered. "We've had the prototype tested in market surveys, and the public loves it."

"Mr. Goldberg," I went on, pointing to a hanging Calder sculpture and other first class art works in his office, " There is no way a person with your good taste can tell me the Richway design is beautiful." It was built anyway, and the yellow mustard walls, with the red and green buttresses. It stayed in the center of town until the chain was bought out by another business, which toned down the building, for which I was thankful. (This site was purchased by the City of Sandy Springs in 2008 for its city hall.)

The outcome of the planning was nil, except to raise general awareness of what was wrong with the present situation. Eventually, we were able to convince Fulton County to make two major moves, which I pushed enthusiastically before the board of commissioners. With the help of then County Attorney Harold Sheats, a sign ordinance was drawn up, with the notable provision that no more rapidly rotating, blinking-and-winking signs would be allowed. We addressed the number and size of future permitted signs in minor ways. Unfortunately, the County never backed the community in our demand that the old signs be removed to meet new standards as new businesses came into Sandy Springs. There was no amortization provision in the ordinances, and as new retailers came in, they just changed the faces on the garish and outsized old signs, without objection from the county.

More significant, perhaps, was the adoption of the tree ordinance, which mandated replanting of trees after commercial development, plus the saving of specimen trees. Commissioner Milton Farris even listened to and acted on my suggestion that the tree ordinance was worthless without an arborist to enforce the law. Energetic Ed Macey was hired and administered the first tree ordinance and its regulations and then shared his ideas with surrounding jurisdictions as they gradually adopted tree ordinances, too. He was one of the few county employees I ever encountered who enforced an ordinance. When a developer violated the tree ordinance, Ed arranged for the developer to donate fourteen good-sized trees that we volunteers then planted along Roswell Road. The biggest problem in this project was securing permission from retail establishments for our tree planting. "Are you sure it will not hide my sign?" they'd inquire. In the meantime, while the ugliness of Roswell Road continued, the county collected an environmental award for passing the tree ordinance.

One notable tree on Roswell Road epitomizes the success of the tree ordinance: the huge oak in the front of the Fountain Oaks shopping center. This was the first specimen saved by the ordinance. A similarly large oak on the site of the present Hammond Springs shopping area was lost before the ordinance was passed, despite efforts by garden club ladies, including Cora Adams, to stand guard to protect the tree.

For many years, devoted environmentalists and garden club enthusiasts would join me in walking Roswell Road and detailing the illegal signs which Fulton County was doing nothing to police. Cora Adams was among them, although at the time she was already reaching "senior" status, and it took all her energy to help measure square footage of signs as we traipsed along the road. We didn't even have the benefit of sidewalks to protect us from the heavy traffic.

At one point we took to the press and issued our list of thirty-one violations. This got the commissioners' attention. But enforcement continued to be sporadic, picking up now and then when a new, ambitious inspector came on force, then gradually deteriorating to the prior levels of frustration. The publicity resulted in my gaining the label "the dragon lady," expressing, I suppose, the opinion of the merchants along the strip.

The focus on signs eventually led to the listing of billboards on Roswell Road. Dr. Harold McPheeters and I presented the county with the list and organized a vociferous group of activists to stop the proliferation of billboards. We had an unexpected ally at the hearing. A small, bespectacled gentleman we did not know rose to speak on our side. He was a stargazing enthusiast and spoke for a group of astronomers who complained that the billboard illumination made it more difficult to view the heavens in the Atlanta area. For once we won, with a final prohibition against any new ones. We still have all the old billboards. Indeed, for a time it became fashionable to embellish the existing billboards with protuberances, such as horns out of a bull to advertise steaks or a car projecting from the sign to push a particular dealer. Again, we argued with no lasting success that this enlargement of surface violated the maximum-size provisions.

The ugliness of the central district, while somewhat mitigated as new establishments show a little more taste, continued to nettle the community. In 1992, I attended the annual budget hearing held in Sandy Springs, mostly a pro forma exercise by the county officials to meet the provisions of their budget laws. Budget hearings in recent years had deteriorated into begging sessions. Instead of the public voicing various priorities for one or another major service, each little special interest group begged for a county grant. This is a result of the county making hundreds of grants for the arts and social services to independent groups, each convinced it is saving the world. In the meantime there is no organized pressure group to seek more policemen or parkland.

At this particular begging session, after hearing the executive director of one group after another asking for funds (and, in effect, his or her salary), I could not stand it anymore. I rose to speak. Michael Lomax was chairman of the commission at the time. "Commissioner Lomax," I said, "I'm not here asking for funds for any particular group—but only for Sandy Springs. This community has been totally neglected. We're one of the busiest commercial arteries in the county, and yet we do not have a sidewalk in the area. Although we've got the highest accident rate of any Fulton County intersection at Roswell Road and I-285, we are stuck with an antiquated left-turn access to the Interstate. (Eighteen years later, this same bridge is still a congestion nightmare. Obtaining state dollars to widen it is the current highest priority on the capital-improvement list for the City of Sandy Springs.) The traffic lights are not coordinated, and the central business district looks like hell. It's time the county undertook a plan to resurrect it, and I request funding for this purpose." Lo and behold, at the end of the meeting Lomax's assistant approached me, "We're going to provide the funds." I had mentioned $75,000—a figure I had pulled out of a hat.

We waited and waited in Sandy Springs. After many months the delay was explained. The only way funds could be appropriated for one area of Fulton County was if a similar expenditure were also made in other areas, regardless of whether or not these other areas experienced the same problem. Eventually $75,000 was appropriated so that each district commissioner could point to an equal grant for his or her constituents.

This grant was the genesis of Sandy Springs Revitalization, Inc. By January 1999 (seven years after I sought the initial funding) only one block of Roswell Road had been transformed. We used county funds to take utility lines to the back of the buildings, to plant trees, to construct a broad sidewalk with brick cross walks, and to erect attractive streetlights. The two corners of the block were even anchored by flower planters and benches. (Since none of the businesses seemed to exert any initiative, I bought pansies and planted them myself, in order to help maintain the decidedly different character of this block.)

The hope was that we could finish at least two more blocks in 1999. The slow pace was frustrating, especially when we compare Sandy Springs to Roswell and Alpharetta, which are just up the highway. There, as municipalities, revitalization is more rapid. Plans are drawn, the community is brought on board, and major areas are revitalized in a short time. The power and financial ability of a city government account for their efficiency versus our slow bumbling progress.

Twice my disgust with Fulton County's disregard for Sandy Springs led to lawsuits. We paid heavy property taxes as well as local sales tax to Fulton County and saw little return for our money. In 1977 the City of Atlanta prevailed on the Georgia Legislature to enact a Special Tax District which levies a special property tax in Sandy Springs and other Fulton unincorporated areas. The idea was to avoid double taxation for the people living in cities like Atlanta. They paid for city services and felt that their county taxes should go for countywide services, and not for municipal-type service, like the county police department, that operates only in the unincorporated areas. Since I had written the definitive methodology for local governments in determining how to avoid such "double taxation," I could not very well object to the enactment of the special service district.

However, when I noted that the funds collected from the special tax on the unincorporated area were being diverted from that area and expended by the county within the City of Atlanta, I rebelled. While the unincorporated area was suffering for lack of parks and other amenities, the county was spending part of our special taxes to provide tennis lessons in inner-city neighborhoods and diverting our dollars for various programs inside Atlanta. (It turned out that the tennis coach providing this service was also the personal tennis coach for the chairman of the Fulton County commission.) By that time the Committee for Sandy Springs had been functioning a good many years in an effort to secure a municipal government for Sandy Springs. We had engaged an Emory law professor who sought a legal angle to overcome the shenanigans of the Georgia General Assembly that rejected our efforts. Failing on that score, Professor Mayton directed our attention to challenging the county on its illegal diversion of our tax dollars, and we won our case in a summary judgment.

Several years later we challenged the county again. For many years homeowners had received garbage pickups via a private company under contract with Fulton County to provide the service, with prisoners from the county prison camp picking up the yard trash. The county decided to close the prison camps, and thus trash pickups went by the wayside. In January 1997, the county then decided to get out of the trash and garbage collection business altogether. They decided to let each homeowner contract personally with a hauler for whatever level of service desired. In Sandy Springs, most of us cherished our backyard pickups and resisted the imposition of curbside pickups as unsightly and cumbersome for the long driveways and hilly terrain in many of our neighborhoods. By privatizing the entire service, the county reasoned that each could choose and pay for whatever level of service desired.

Sometime later it came to my attention that the commissioner representing South Fulton County had prevailed on the board to reinstitute trash pickups in South Fulton. We on the north end would pay for the service in private fees. On the south end the county provided the service, paid for with mostly our tax dollars. I saw red and went ballistic. First I warned the county I would not sit idly by, and then followed up on this threat by engaging a lawyer who prepared the suit.

Loud wailing and consternation ensued at the board of commissioners. Finally they voted to adopt the principle that, beginning with the next fiscal year, everyone would be treated the same. I withdrew the lawsuit, figuring I had won. But this rejoicing was premature. As January 1999 approached, the commissioner whose district enjoyed the free trash pickups reinserted into the proposed county budget sufficient revenues to fund the service on his end of the county alone. Again, I raised my voice, using the Committee of Sandy Springs as the vehicle. We won the principle when the county inserted into the budget a commensurate amount (on a per-capita basis) for "environmental enhancement."

That meant that on the North side we could use the extra funds for revitalization or park acquisition, while on the south end they could still have trash pickups provided via the county. I reasoned that the firms now contracting with the homeowners in Sandy Springs to haul both garbage and trash would probably fail to reduce their rates if the trash pickups were eliminated. Thus the community would be better off with the extra allocation in the county budget for "environmental enhancements" which otherwise would not have been secured. As it turned out, Sandy Springs did procure several projects (including some sidewalks) from this extra allocation, which became known as "The Trash Money."

Of course, legal action would not be cheap and required constant money raising. We formed a sister organization, Citizens for Sandy Springs, a 501(c)(3) non-profit organization that could receive tax-exempt donations. The "Citizens" could not lobby, but could provide educational materials and pursue legal action. Tibby deJulio, who had been on board the Committee for Sandy Springs for several years, became the president of Citizens for Sandy Springs.

We emphasized the argument that we were totally disenfranchised by the local courtesy rule in the General Assembly, whereby our bill always died in the Fulton delegation. We raised funds twice with gala affairs and silent auctions, while maintaining a fairly regular schedule of fund-raising letters to supporters in Sandy Springs.

Our first venture into the courts came in response to an attorney who contacted us: Keegan Federal. Senator Sallie Newbill and I visited with him several times, exploring possible causes for action, but this attempt failed. Our next start was with Ed Wheeler, who came highly recommended by Arthur K. Bolton, a former State Attorney General of Georgia. Mr. Wheeler enthusiastically filed suits naming every big leader of the General Assembly and included charges of violations of the RICO act—i.e. racketeering. The filings were fairly preposterous and unsophisticated. Everything was being run on a shoestring; Tibby deJulio even delivered the charges personally to various defendants.

This suit did not serve us well. Mr. Wheeler, besides serving as attorney, also operated an avant-garde restaurant (The Green Crocodile, if I remember correctly) and fairly soon severed his ties with us as he gained a federal appointment to an administrative judgeship. The suit was retracted.

After repeated rebuffing by the General Assembly, we felt compelled to continue down the judicial route, and eventually were very ably represented by Michael Bowers. He had recently retired as Georgia's Attorney General and had just lost a spirited gubernatorial race. Mr. Bowers had a strong Constitutional background and honed in on the "one-man, one vote" issue that had overturned the notorious county-unit system of Georgia. His argument showed that the local delegations, in whose hands our referendum issue repeatedly died, did not follow the one man-one vote rule. For example a representative on the Fulton delegation (Billy McKinney) had only one or two precincts of his district in Fulton County, but he had the same vote on the delegation as representatives all of whose districts are situated in the county. This arrangement prevailed in the local delegations of the Georgia House and Senate throughout the state.

Unfortunately, neither the United States District Court nor the Court of Appeals saw the issue in the same way. The great resistance of courts to interfere in the operations of the legislative branch no doubt played a role in these rulings. Our suit was appealed to the Supreme Court of the United States, which declined to review it. We went all the way to no avail. We were thrown back upon the vicissitudes of the Georgia General Assembly.

This same representative, Billy McKinney, had played a fairly important role over the years in denying passage of our bills. He chaired the delegation, and his daughter, Representative Cynthia McKinney (then a State representative—later a notorious United States Representative) was appointed to a subcommittee of the delegation to consider the Sandy Springs bill.

We felt it was important to show Representative McKinney that Sandy Springs was a decent community where the races get along. We invited her to visit Highpoint Elementary School, which had almost equal enrollment of whites and blacks. (There were few Hispanics in Sandy Springs at that time.) She happened to arrive at the school into the principal's office just as he was ministering to a black little girl lying on a sofa and resting. He told us the child occasionally suffers from epileptic spells and that the staff had been trained to deal with her condition. He was calming her while waiting for her working mother to reach the school. If this event had been staged, it could not have been a stronger emotional exhibition of wonderful human relations. Cynthia was visibly impressed.

I later assisted her by talking to my neighbor, a private school principal, as Cynthia was attempting to remove her child from public school. The outcome of all this was that Cynthia reported our bill out of her subcommittee favorably, only to have it shot down when her father handled it with the full committee.

My battles with the county are a manifestation of the alienation Sandy Springs feels from the distant, non-responsive type of government that was never meant to provide municipal-type services. That alienation accounts for the formation of the Committee for Sandy Springs to secure local government for the area.

Seeing the World

One of the great plusses of John's academic career was the opportunity it afforded us to travel. He was forever going to meetings, not just in the United States, but also to Europe and beyond. Since his expenses were paid, this translated into a reduced vacation cost for the two of us. I accompanied him to Europe for the first time in 1962. In preparation I poured over *Europe on $5 a Day*, (it is now *Europe on $85 a Day*), and we stayed in simple pensions or small hotels, eating with the locals. The children were still young, and we employed a wonderful baby sitter, Mrs. Claypool, to stay with them, which alleviated some of my worrying. I did not learn, until our first return from Europe four weeks after the event that Tobae had fallen out of a tree days after our departure, and Dr. Patterson, the pediatrician, had been called to check her out. In later years, we would manage to find summer camps for the children while I joined John in Europe.

We covered a lot of territory that first trip in 1962, beginning in Paris, through Italy and Switzerland and to Hungary to visit John's father. On our many subsequent trips to Europe, we almost always included Zermatt, Switzerland—our favorite destination. Indeed, on one of our trips, with John preceding me to attend his meeting, I joined him in Zermatt and we set out immediately for a hiking trail even after my sleepless transatlantic flight and train ride. We were avid hikers, and managed twice to reach the "hutte"— the stop where the real Alpiners sleep before their early morning ascent to the peak of the Matterhorn.

Italy was another favorite, from the Alps down through Tuscany, and from Rome, along the Amalfi coast, into Sicily. We liked the Italian spirit, the trattorias, and the scenery. We spent less time in the museums than on trails or streets, absorbing the atmosphere.

On my first return to Europe since our family had moved to the United States, we included a stop in Genoa. I wanted my husband to see where I had spent such happy childhood years. We found the apartment building on the Atto Venucci, which still looked nice, and took the elevator to the penthouse, and, with some apprehension, rang the doorbell. A very surprised Italian couple came to the door and seemed quite taken aback by these brash Americans who came uninvited to see the apartment. I tried my broken Italian, as well as German and college French, and together with hand motions somehow eventually we got through to them that I had lived there as a child— *"quando piccola bambina"*—and wanted to revisit the apartment. Then they graciously allowed us to look around. The terrazzo floors were even more beautiful than I had remembered. The terrace still gave a view of the fabulous panorama of the sea and mountains. It was still a wonderful place, and I was not disappointed.

My reaction was totally different, however, when we revisited Nervi, the immediate suburb to the south of Genoa on the Riviera. Instead of the heavenly scent of mimosa, we encountered the fumes of motorcycles everywhere. The boardwalk along the cliffs was littered and crowded. To some extent the difference lay in the fact that more and more local residents could now access the beautiful sites, as is of course true of most tourist destinations in the world. Portofino, on the other hand, was just as I had remembered it, since the residents are determined not to allow any changes, and they have limited motor access. Santa Margherita, where we stayed high above the cliffs by the Mediterranean Sea, also lived up to the lushness and serenity of my romantic memories.

One of our most memorable stays was at the Villa Caruso in Ravello, high above the Amalfi drive. The Villa Caruso was world famous for a delicious brandy soufflé, which capped the nightly dinner. I tried to replicate it at home, but never succeeded. My parents had been enamored of Southern Italy and visited Mr. Caruso's establishment on their trips, so when John and I went, we, of course, mentioned my parents. "Oh, that simpatico professore!" he exclaimed and insisted that we carry a complimentary bottle of the wine from his vineyard across the rest of our trip as a present for Dad. When Tobae and her husband were in Europe we then recommended Caruso's, and they were the third generation to be enchanted with the charming villa and its peaceful view of the sparsely inhabited valleys that spill out on the rocky Mediterranean coast.

Good food is central to our memories of travel in Italy. We had our most memorable meal on a stop in Syracuse as we sailed from Lisbon to Alexandria, Egypt, on the Funchal cruise ship. The cruise was a traveling liver meeting. While John lectured occasionally, I amused myself with bridge games, which were conducted totally in Portuguese, but that did not seem to matter.

A local group of doctors met the ship in Syracuse and took us on a sightseeing tour. The central square still featured a temporary platform where yesterday's political meeting had been held. The colors were all bright red—this was the heyday of communism in Southern Italy. The mayor, with the insignia of his office hanging from his neck, gave our group a short welcome within City Hall, and then it was off to lunch in a local restaurant.

If only we had known that the first three courses of pasta, each with delicious seafood, were only appetizers! By the time the main courses and desserts were served, along with liters of good wine, we were almost unable to move. We staggered through the hot sunshine back to the boat, eager to lie down.

On later trips, while John was attending international conferences, I enjoyed the entertainments provided by the local host committees. I found the contrast between the typical ladies' program of a conference in America (which usually involved shopping in boutiques) and those held in other countries notable. One memorable ladies' tour, for example, involved a visit to a foundation established by a wealthy Swiss family. The library in the Lake Geneva waterfront villa contained ancient documents from monasteries, with lustrous illustrations along the borders of the pages, as well as one of the few surviving Gutenberg Bibles.

In Kanazawa, Japan, the local host committee took the ladies to a modern museum that included collections of ancient Japanese art. The pictures in which Japanese make-up for women included a great deal of black decoration were especially striking. From the more modern exhibits, we learned that Japanese brides do not yearn for a service of matched china, but rather individually produced and decorated bowls. At the formal banquet, which concluded the meeting, everyone's place setting was an individual work of art. The guests were regaled with a memento: two sake cups hand-produced by a contemporary artist.

One of John's fellows in gastroenterology lived in Kyoto and entertained us royally. This included a traditional Japanese dinner in a restaurant where our party sat in a private room on pillows around a low table. I suffered terribly because I had on a narrow skirt, which made sitting this way quite difficult. The food came in a multitude of small courses, each presented with gorgeous bowls and trays, usually with a blossom to adorn the dish. The highlight of the trip for me was the visit to the major gardens of Kyoto, where they practice the true art of landscaping. The trees are bent to a particular shape over the years, and each bend in the trail opens to yet another peaceful and graceful vista. In one garden, we came upon a group of Japanese schoolgirls who were very anxious to try their English on us—and did so, with many giggles.

My trip to Japan with John came during a time when the United States was particularly concerned with the trade imbalance with Japan. We were worried that the Japanese manufacturing plants were supplanting American products, while the Japanese refused to accept American goods. I put my foot in my mouth one morning at breakfast when I remarked, "Smucker's jams! I have finally found an import from America." There was a long silence, and eventually one of the Japanese hosts asked what manufacturer had produced the airplane in which we had traveled. (It was a Boeing, of course.)

In Majorca, the local entertainment committee had arranged for the conference to eat in an old fort at the top of the hill. The guests were allowed to perch along the thick walls and porticos where lookouts were posted in ancient days to protect Majorca from invaders. The evening culminated with a presentation of folk dancing from the different regions in Spain, each with characteristic costumes and exciting music.

Yet another unforgettable event as part of an international liver meeting took place at a villa near Padua, Italy, which had once been owned by Vivaldi's patron. We were treated to a chamber music concert of Vivaldi compositions as we sat in the main hall of this villa, where the composer had written the pieces. The banquet was later served in the lower level, the walls of which were finished in a most unusual style: seashells were embedded into the entire façade of the walls.

A traveling exhibit on the history of medicine was the highlight of the visit to Padua. Fascinating displays traced the progress in various specialties, especially surgery, complete with an assortment of dreadful instruments used through the centuries. Those used for amputations, as well as the various prostheses developed over the years, attracted many viewers.

The University of Padua is ancient and renowned as the institution where Galileo and Vesalius taught. The latter is considered the father of anatomy, and the exhibit demonstrated the differences between his anatomical descriptions versus the ancient ones by Galen. We visited the amphitheater that had been used since the 1500s, with steep wooden galleries, where the medical students leaned perilously over the railings to observe the professor dissecting a cadaver far below in the center. The dissection of cadavers was prohibited in the 1500s. The dissecting table could tilt, in case the public authorities were imminent, and the body would be disposed of into a stream that ran below the aperture of the dissecting table. In another part of the old medical school, we were shown how the faculty would sit at a u-shaped table to quiz a medical student before he could graduate. What a far cry from computerized testing!

In 1969, all five of us went to Europe. Tobae was fifteen, Johnny fourteen, and Michael eleven years old. We were alternately taken aback and amused by their teenage foibles. Tobae discovered boys that trip. In a Danish town where the American Navy was berthed to celebrate the Fourth of July, she momentarily disappeared below decks with a sailor. Then in Helsingor, Denmark, while I attended a medical dinner with John, the children were instructed to buy hamburgers. When we returned, Tobae had disappeared. The boys reported she had met a Danish sailor who walked her to the docks. I was frantic. We walked up and down the street asking everyone, "Have you seen a girl with yellow pants and long black hair?" She turned up and hour or so later, having ridden the ferry to Sweden and back with her new acquaintance. We were beside ourselves. When we visited the castle in Salzburg, we paid special attention to the exhibit with the chastity belts used in the medieval days, and promised she would be tied into one if she ever strayed again.

Johnny exhibited his hormones differently. He gravitated to the kiosks where they sold magazines. Many weeks later at home we found the girlie magazines he had bought hidden under his bed. He apparently invited the neighbor boys for special viewings.

We met my sister Marianne and her family in Zermatt, so that the dignified and quiet dining room of the Hotel Perren was transformed into a lively American scene. The six children sat at one table, and we sat at another. The cousins had a wonderful time together, and all managed to reach the hutte on the Matterhorn. Every afternoon the kids enjoyed the special treat of going to the *Konditorei* to pick out their individual pastries.

In Zermatt we had to contend with the rising hormones again. Tobae attracted the attention of the blond, apple-cheeked waiter who served their table, who asked her to go to the town square after dinner. "Please, please, let me go." I looked at the young man, and shrugged, figuring he was just an innocent Swiss country boy. That was not quite the reality. He turned out to be Italian and for several months Tobae would receive cards from him asking if he could come to America.

It was inevitable that travel to Europe in the 1970s would be inconvenienced because of strikes. One trip to Rome on Alitalia was horrible because the toilets on the airplane had not been cleaned. Once we sat in Zurich for many hours when a strike in France had disrupted all the schedules. The most memorable result of labor unrest came when we left London, and shortly after the departure the captain announced, "We will be landing in Uganda, because the air traffic controllers are on a slowdown at Kennedy Airport in New York." "My God," I screamed to John. "What are we doing going to Uganda?" This was during the days of the dictator Idi Amin, shortly after the Israelis commandos had successfully rescued the passengers of a hijacked plane in that country. In fact, the Italian headlines had screamed "Israelis in Uganda." I laboriously translated the story in an effort to comprehend why the Israelis were in Uganda, of all places.

Well, it turned out that I had only had Uganda on the brain, and the captain had really announced we would land in Gander, Newfoundland, to refuel, in case Kennedy would not let us land right away. Gander was bleak and barren. It had been developed as an airport during World War II for American bombers to take off in their raids against Germany. When we reached the coast off New York, the traffic controllers had apparently settled their dispute, and we were given clearance to land. We had to circle over the Atlantic for quite a while to dump the extra fuel before landing. Somehow when the pilot does this, it gives the feeling of added thrust, which is disquieting to uninformed passengers.

Adventures of an Economist

At a certain point, I recognized that the urge to be back in the work world had been building for quite a while. Finally, when Michael was in kindergarten in 1963, I took a part time job on the staff of then Georgia Governor Sanders's task force to improve education in Georgia. This was half research and half propaganda. The object was to prove that the legislature needed to spend more to educate Georgians for economic progress.

The most notable output of that research effort was a graph highlighting "ghost jobs." The colored shapes on the graph represented jobs that could be filled, and the blank, "ghost" shapes stood for those that could not be filled because we lacked a sufficiently large number of educated and trained people. The "ghost jobs" became a fairly popular element of the task-force output.

After the Sanders task force, I gravitated to a teaching position at Clark College on the Atlanta University campus. I began as a liberal, but the experience of trying to teach unprepared students beginning economics was the start of my realization that the system wasn't working. My students were totally incapable of following the lessons. They could not comprehend the textbook; they could not distinguish between the words "corporation" and "cooperation." I felt I was failing to interest them in the subject.

In the early 1960s, there were still few professional opportunities for black college graduates. Many of the women graduates would end up teaching in the school system, which was still segregated. I felt it important to encourage the students and expose them to the United States Civil Service exams, since government was one venue that was definitely open to them, regardless of their race. Therefore, I urged the administration to have the students take the test, if for nothing more than to experience a taste of the competitive world. I was totally blocked because the deans felt it would be traumatic for the students to take these tests. They didn't believe in challenging the students at all. For an entire year, I taught three days per week, and tried to make friends with other faculty, but only encountered a wall. I eventually became discouraged and decided that perhaps teaching at Georgia State University would be different. I had taught labor problems there in 1950, when it was a night division of the University of Georgia. When I approached the chairman of the economics department, he encouraged me to enroll in the Ph.D. program, with my tuition paid as a graduate assistant, to qualify me for college teaching.

Although I was dimly aware that I enjoyed advocacy and analysis, I still veered away from law school, which in those days would have meant either Emory University or non-university-affiliated private law programs. Emory tuition was high, and I certainly did not want to add that cost to the family budget. As the daughter of a law professor at the University of Georgia, the non-academic law schools seemed below my dignity. So, instead, in 1965, I enrolled in the Ph.D. program in economics at Georgia State University.

The chairman told me that to prepare for the required calculus course, I should brush up on algebra. I can't pin it down for sure: it was either a University of Chicago or Encyclopedia Britannica self-taught algebra course that I studied during the summer. Day after day, while watching the kids swim, I sat by the pool working through algebra problems and differential equations. By the end of the summer, I thought I was well prepared, so I was unpleasantly surprised when I began calculus. All but two of us students were men, many of whom had studied calculus before at Georgia Tech. To me it was incomprehensible at first, and I would come home in tears. The timing of the courses was no help. The calculus course was at five in the evening, which meant returning to downtown Atlanta for the evening class, with some horrible dinner warming in the oven, ready for the children.

John not only put up with all this, he also came to my rescue. He would work the calculus problems with me, and the veil gradually lifted. By the end of the year, the content made sense, and I was doing okay.

Economics seemed quite different by then from what I had learned in the 1940s. Current economists were challenging the Keynes philosophy, which had guided so much of the New Deal. For the first time, I read Adam Smith in the original, and encountered the logic of the "invisible hand" in his inimitable exposition. The Stigler school of the University of Chicago was another new insight and the more I learned, the more I realized that centralized decision making and planning of the economy did not produce optimum solutions.

Each student had to choose two specialties, and I gravitated to "labor problems" and "urban finance." The former built on the master's program of earlier years, and the latter dovetailed into my growing interest in the intricacies of local government. My thesis was certainly no monumental new offering, but it gave me a firm grounding on tax-base analysis, which would come in handy in later years.

I did a good bit of my studying for the academic courses in the car. The children were at the age to take all kinds of lessons. So I was driving them to a variety of activities; the back of the station wagon was my library. While waiting for their activities to end, I studied. I didn't want to lose a minute.

By 1968, I thought I had finished the thesis, but things did not work out that way. One of my three thesis advisors left Atlanta to teach at a different institution, but posed a number of questions before he left. (He had never communicated with me about any of the chapters before then.) The matter was resolved when a new advisor was appointed, but, of course, the graduation deadline for 1968 was shot. I made a few changes in 1969, and I finally earned the degree that year. Graduation epitomized the constant schedule conflicts in our lives. Tobae's piano recital was at the same time as the graduation, and I would have to miss being there for her.. So we divided our forces, and John attended the recital while I collected my parchment. Morris Abrams, a prominent figure in Washington, was the commencement speaker, and although he never seemed friendly when we were students together at the University of Georgia, he was especially cordial to me as I marched across the stage to pick up the diploma.

All through the 1968-69 academic year, I was already picking up consulting jobs. This was a period of federal largesse, which was good for economists as many grants projects required economic analysis. I could not have come along at a better time. One of the first projects I worked on involved an analysis of the Georgia Department of Revenue. I just marched in to the director and suggested the need for tying together the taxpayers' records in the various divisions. I got my first contract. About the same time, I somehow landed a consulting job on something totally uneconomic: designing sensitivity training for teachers as the Atlanta school system embarked on integration. Concurrently, I picked up a contract that dealt with impoverished Northwest Georgia counties, with proposals to help them develop.

Over the next sixteen years, the consulting jobs gradually increased so that often I was juggling several projects at the same time. My half-time position on the research staff of the Southern Regional Education Board (SREB) allowed a lot of flexibility. I could make up times when I was absent on consulting. I also found that I usually got more done in the half-time position at SREB than the fulltime staffers accomplished, so nobody objected to absences for other work. Some consulting assignments were pretty tedious, such as drafting new business-license ordinances for local governments. I tended to push licenses based on gross receipts of businesses and succeeded in getting Fulton County to adopt this method. In the many years since this happened, the county has collected millions that they wouldn't have otherwise. Sandy Springs inherited this business-license method when I became mayor of the new city. Many businesses in Sandy Springs often complain about the burden of the license tax, but few know I was the one who drafted it.

Other projects were more interesting. A partnership with Art Schreiber and Sam Skogstad of the economics department at Georgia State attracted quite a bit of consulting work. With our almost nonexistent overhead, we could underbid established consulting firms. We did our work in our respective offices and burned the midnight oil.

During the 1970s the grant spigot was pouring freely from Washington, and some of it flowed our way. Our partnership, The Institute for Government and Economic Research, received a grant to prepare a publication that provided practical hints for local government officials on how to apply economic analysis in running their counties and cities. Its subtitle, "Making Sense out of Dollars," was illustrated on the cover by a stream of pennies pouring out of a budget ledger. The publication led to another grant: to make oral pitches to conferences of local government officials. Since any conference entails the securing of speakers to fill a schedule, we were soon in demand across the country to attend state conventions of city and county elected and administrative people.

With their teaching responsibilities, my Georgia State partners were reluctant to travel too far, so I was assigned California and Alaska, among others. In November, 1979, I jetted to Fairbanks to a conference whose attendees were all flown in on expense accounts. (All budgets in Alaska include air transport, since it's practically the only way to get around in that state.) Most of these officials had more immediate concerns in running their towns than to apply economic theory to their problems, but they listened politely.

For the trip to Fairbanks, I pulled out my ancient mouton coat from the days at the University of Illinois and borrowed boots. I was determined to see as much as possible, and on arrival immediately located a bush pilot to fly me around the next day. A retired U. S. Air Force pilot picked me up the next morning, while it was still dark. As he parked the car on a snowed-in parking lot and plugged it into a heater, I saw the little single-engine Cessna on skis in which we would fly.

"Let me show you the survival gear in the back," my pilot announced, as we prepared to embark. By eleven, there was sufficient sunshine, which, combined with the clear air and the pervasive snow everywhere, created a brilliant scene. We took off and soon were flying at 13,000 feet around Mount McKinley. Tourists often miss the mountain on summer visits because of clouds and fog. I had a perfect view. Soon, however,

I clamored, "I'm feeling dizzy, please get me lower." Flying at lower altitudes, the pilot pointed to what seemed like match sticks across the expanse of white: the Alaskan oil pipeline. Eventually, flying ever lower, we spotted a moose or two, which made the tour perfect. By three I was back in the hotel, and it was turning dark.

Two consulting assignments grew out of the planning for rapid transit in Atlanta. One of the major issues was the question of funding a system. My job was to analyze various possible revenue sources. Among them, of course, was a potential sales tax, which I described as regressive, by placing a greater burden on a poor household than a wealthier one. Yet this is exactly the source that was chosen for the referendum on rapid transit. I believe it was Mayor Sam Massell who floated the sales tax as the method of financing rail, coupled with the proposal that the fare would be only fifteen cents. In some ways, this was quite clever. The tax was regressive, but the people most likely to ride the system would benefit from the highly subsidized fare. Today the fare is up to two dollars, and it is still a highly subsidized fare. (State law provided that fares must cover a minimum of forty-five percent of the operating cost of the system.)

My other involvement in the rapid transit system came when I had to suggest likely economic uses for the land around the proposed rail stops. Various economists were assigned different stations. I drew some very unglamorous ones: Garnett Street, Hightower Street, Avondale Estates, and West End. The supposition was that the crowds attracted to the stations for transport would also bring opportunities for retail and office uses. Most of that has not come to pass in the stations I was assigned. The catch was that when several developers were all using the same buying power and population projections to justify their individual projects, they were all using the same demand, which couldn't possibly stretch to cover multiple projects for the same buying power. I believe that was one of the reasons there was so much overbuilding in the 1980s. The banks that financed too many projects did not pay attention to the common-sense feedback from the general public about overbuilding.

Under contract with the Georgia Municipal Association (GMA), it was my job to do the research to back up the proposals that it was promoting in the state legislature. For example, we documented unmet needs and service requirements of cities throughout the state to justify the need for a local option sales tax. We compared Georgia property tax burdens with other states, to show the need for a diversification of local revenues.

It was an opportunity to really learn the politics of city and state relationships and the legislative process. Elmer George, Executive Director of the GMA, was a dynamic leader. When he zeroed in on an issue, he truly hammered it in, and he organized relentless advocacy on the part of city officials to lobby their local legislators. Statewide annual meetings in Savannah or Jekyll Island featured highly anticipated receptions that attracted huge attendance. I began to learn the art of lobbying.

A memorable assignment from GMA was to represent the cities' interests at a Georgia Public Service rate hearing. The issue was that street lighting, an expense of cities, is an off-peak load on the electric system, and, therefore, does not impinge on capacity, usually the major cost element in rate hearings. In order to prepare myself for the hearing, I checked out books on rate making from Georgia Tech. When I presented my findings using the technical terms I had picked up in the textbooks, the opposing attorney (Carl Sanders, a former governor of Georgia) turned to his assistant, Norman Underwood, and I could hear him whisper, "What is she talking about?" (Mr. Underwood eventually served on the Georgia Supreme Court.) Anyhow, GMA won the case, and the rates for street lighting were reduced. I joked that I should have undertaken the assignment on a commission based on the cities' utility savings.

The project that probably gave me the most satisfaction grew out of my work at the Southern Regional Education Board (SREB). One of the recurrent waves of educational reform that swept the country took place in the early 1980s, and I was on the leading edge. SREB had been formed as a consortium of Southern states in the late 1940s to improve higher education. By 1980 it became clear that the quality of colleges and universities hinged on the product of the high schools, and so on down the line. So SREB embarked on a reform drive for public education.

I headed the staff that prepared the report for the South, calling for stiffer high-school graduation standards, for teacher testing, and higher admission standards for the colleges of education. Our report predated the national one, "A Nation at Risk," which made the same points, but, of course, garnered a lot more attention.

In the years to come at SREB, I published and testified before legislative and academic groups on details regarding teacher education. A study of some 2,000 college graduates' transcripts compared the level and content of the subjects taken by arts-and-science majors versus teacher-education graduates. The results were a scathing indictment of the colleges of education, which certainly disagreed with everything I had to say. Now, sixteen years later, with another wave of educational reform, I note an echo of this message. In Georgia, for example, a recent chancellor of the university system is leading a change to arts-and-science content in teacher education.

Another facet of education that caught my attention was vocational education in the high schools. It became apparent that it was a dumping ground, and that often it lacked rigor. I certainly had no argument against preparing some students for work straight out of high school, instead of pushing everyone into colleges. Yet the huge vocational education enrollments in home economics and cosmetics for the girls and wood shop for the boys made no sense to me. Eventually an assignment came my way: The Advisory Board to the United States Center on Vocational Education in Ohio. I took it seriously, determined not to be a yes-person for an agenda predetermined by vocational educators. I needled and fumed at the periodic meetings of the advisory board about the weak offerings of vocational education. The center director had been accustomed to setting the agenda for the meetings, and I objected, pointing out that it was the function of the board to determine what it wanted to discuss. The vocational-education community did not appreciate me either, needless to say.

When preparing early drafts of the reform report at SREB, I did inject some paragraphs referring to rising numbers enrolled in private schools. Mentioning vouchers directly was not even on my horizon at the time. But even the reference to private schools was removed from subsequent drafts as possibly offensive to the education establishment. There have been so many reform commissions and reports, but so little improvement. The public school establishment's only remedy is the same old one— more dollars are the cure. After the vast increases in public funding, I am more than ever convinced that competition and choice are the required medicine to improve K-12 education.

At about this time I was really on board with the Republican philosophy and determined that perhaps I should make a substantial contribution to the second-term campaign for Ronald Reagan. Paul Coverdell was then a state senator representing my district, and I asked him, "How would a $1,000 contribution make the most impact to my eventually getting an assignment on some board on public policy?" Paul said he would take care of it. "I'll make sure it goes to the right party." I was surely surprised that this party turned out to be the campaign fund for George Bush, candidate for vice-president. Paul had always been extremely close to Bush, and I still have a picture in which I have a scowl on my face as Bush shakes my hand. (I don't think I meant to make such a mean impression.)

Eventually a call came from the personnel office of the White House inquiring whether I would be interested in a job as a deputy under Secretary of Education to deal with vocational education. This would have entailed living in Washington, D.C., and commuting back and forth to Atlanta. It was not a difficult decision to say no. I gradually tired of working for SREB. I felt its major thrust on reforming K-12 was finished. The lavish expenditure by SREB on fancy meetings at expensive resorts for the governors and legislators who funded SREB seemed excessive to me. I questioned why SREB was treading so hard on K-12 while ignoring the waste and academic decay that permeated so much of higher education. Also, my beloved direct boss, Tex Scheitinger, retired about this time, and was replaced by a young man for whom I had no respect at all. (He only lasted about six months, before the Board of Regents hired him, where he also did not last too long.)

At about this time, a gift arrived in the office for me from the Governor of Louisiana. It was a large, high-quality, framed Audubon print, perfect for a traditional décor, but not my contemporary house. (I had done some testifying in Louisiana to legislators about teacher education and vocational education. I always wondered what the source was for Audubon prints that Governor Edwards apparently sent to consultants.) I met with the President of SREB, Winfred Godwin, and said, "I have good news and bad news. The good news is that I am donating the Audubon print to SREB for its new building, and the bad news is that I am resigning." So I forged out on my own on education consulting projects. I had the most fun with the one that focused on the layers and layers of administrators and service personnel in higher education.

Dad and I had often talked about the changes he had witnessed at the University of Georgia Law School. At first there was a dean with one secretary and the faculty. As the years passed, this metamorphosed into assistant deans, placement officers, alum liaisons, public-relations people, development officers, and other non-teaching positions. My association with higher education through SREB had awakened an awareness of the tremendous overload of non-teaching personnel in higher education. (Research, however, is, I believe, an integral part of the teaching function and a fundamental component of higher education.)

William Bennett, then the United States Secretary of Education, and his assistant, Checker Finn, were aware of my work on education reform and were instrumental in funding a study whereby I would focus on two higher-education systems to determine just what proportion of the total staff served the traditional objective of teaching and research. I had picked the entire public higher-education system of Florida, because all its personnel were on a computerized data system, and the University of Georgia, where I wanted to do an on-site analysis of the total professional staff.

The University of Georgia part of this project started off rocky. I visited Interim President of the University Stanford, and explained that I wanted to find out what all the administrative personnel functions were.

He replied, "I've always wanted to know what all the deans and assistant deans do." However, the project had to be approved by the University Council. Not unexpectedly, they nixed any review of their functions.

Not long before, the University of Georgia had been embroiled in a major public scandal on firing Jan Kemp, a teacher who insisted that football players complete remedial studies. She was eventually vindicated, and the University of Georgia had some egg on its face. I went to the same lawyer she used and asked him to apply the Freedom of Information Act to the data I needed for my analysis. This he did, and his work produced the desired records.

One of the results of this study was a reduction of Agricultural Extension Service personnel attached to the College of Agriculture at the University of Georgia. In Fulton County, the Extension Service helped gardeners such as me in identifying plant diseases or planning flowerbeds. I wondered why such a function should be underwritten by the state, through the University of Georgia. The heavy support of extension agents was a legacy from the time when the state was much more dependent on agriculture. This situation illustrated how difficult it is to ever get rid of an outdated function once it becomes embedded through government financing.

Labor arbitration was another aspect of my professional work. I approached Joe Jacobs, who had long represented labor legally, and who had introduced me to my first employer, the *Atlanta Journal of Labor*. "Could you get me on the roster of labor arbitrators of the Federal Mediation and Conciliation Board?" Joe helped immediately. In the 1970s, federal agencies were beginning their efforts to incorporate women in professional jobs. I was named to the roster. The first case was one that involved the Jacobs law firm, and I was never very proud of my efforts. Joe's son practically wrote the labor award for me. But from that time on, I was totally independent, and have thoroughly enjoyed applying what Dad always said were my legal talents to interpreting contracts and clauses.

For several years, until Florida decided it had more than enough retired labor experts living within its own boundaries, I served on a panel that recommended solutions when labor and public agencies could not agree on new contracts. Sometimes I would appear at the scene and the entire labor contract was up for grabs. Nothing was agreeable to either party. In other situations, only one or two clauses were at stake. The special master, as I was called, made a recommendation for a solution and a rationale for that position, which was published in a local paper. Yet, for the most part, the special-master recommendations were not implemented. They did serve to defuse the situation, and, of course, to avoid strikes in the public sector.

During the 1990s, as labor unions represented a shrinking portion of private-sector employment, more and more of the cases assigned to me involved government workers. They argued incessantly over minute matters, and their agreements were terribly convoluted and detailed, as compared to most private-sector situations. It became abundantly clear in this period that it was very difficult for a government agency to discipline an employee.

Cancer

In 1982, two years before I left SREB, I had breast cancer. I found the lump myself, and asked John to feel it. He immediately made an appointment with a breast-cancer specialist at Emory, and I was scheduled for exploratory surgery in two weeks. Regular mammograms had not revealed anything. I checked into the hospital the day before surgery and was totally ignored while I lay on the floor because I suffered from backaches. That resulted in more tests and x-rays, as the staff ruled out the spread into any bones. Indeed, the tests I underwent were endless and entailed being totally still while rotating on stainless steel tables with strange machinery overhead.

When I woke from surgery, I became aware that I had undergone a mastectomy. In retrospect, I think the medical personnel knew all along what would happen, but left the patient with the hope that maybe it was a false alarm. In those days, one was allowed at least a week in the hospital, so that by the time I came home, I felt quite well. My major concern was cosmetic, and soon I was on the phone contacting firms that manufactured various types of prostheses. I do not recall any particular fears about life expectancy. At first I just figured: it's done with, now I can get on with my life. I was back in the pool within three weeks, exercising my arm to make sure I suffered no restriction in movement. The worst inconvenience seemed to be not driving for four weeks and losing my independence in that way. Then it hit me: I was to undergo chemotherapy for six months.

John had not informed me after surgery that I had positive lymph glands, but insisted I undergo chemotherapy as a precaution. Of course, when I had my first appointment with the oncologist, they spilled the beans: "You know that you had positive lymph nodes."

The fear of losing my hair was worse than any other part of the ordeal. The chemotherapy would lay me really low for a day or so after each treatment, but then I would spring back, and go about work at SREB and the private consulting. For some reason, I was told to eat a good breakfast before the chemo treatment. So John and I visited the Emory cafeteria for a full breakfast. For many years, the smell of bacon made me sick, as it reminded me of the impending chemo treatments.

The possible hair loss really bothered me. Looking back, I was totally ridiculous. I ceased to brush my hair, in fear of loosening it, and I would wear scarves to protect my hair against the wind pulling it out. Just in case, I ordered a hairpiece I could wear if needed. All these fears were unfounded. I was one of the lucky ones, and in those days the drug now used that is almost certain to cause hair loss was not part of the package.

Eighteen months after the mastectomy, I had reconstructive surgery, and I never had to worry again about wearing a bathing suit or a low-cut gown. When all the scare stuff came out about breast implants, I filled out the forms honestly: I had no bad symptoms, but I had been implanted with the products on the list of various suits. In succeeding years, as these suits made their way through the courts, I received two checks: one for $1,000 from the 3-M company and one for $2,500 from the Dow Corporation. I felt a little guilty about receiving these as a result of the class-action suits, but deposited them nevertheless.

Thirteen years after the mastectomy, I had another scare: a bronchoscopy showed cancer in the lungs. Yet the surgeon remarked to John that what he saw was not a typical lung cancer, and John said, "Well, you know, she had breast cancer thirteen years ago. Could it be a recurrence?" Perhaps typical of surgeons, when I went to an office visit prior to the procedure, he did not take my history. He did not know I had had breast cancer before. Luckily, with John's medical school connections, it was possible to retrieve the old slides of the breast cancer in 1982 and to compare them to what was found in 1995. Yes, it was a recurrence of the same cancer.

Martin York, the oncologist, put me on tamoxifen, and counseled, "If this does not work, we have other drugs." I can't say I was put into a terrible downward spiral of fear and anguish. I resented the symptoms that getting used to tamoxifen brought on, and possibly that was a disguise of deeper fear. But, generally, my attitude was "Hell, I'm going on with my life, and nobody is going to know about this." As a treat, John and I planned a getaway to Chateau Frontenac in Quebec and then a cruise on a small boat up the St. Lawrence River.

This was one of our best trips. We relished each other, the golden autumn scenery along the banks of the river, and the carefree, leisurely sightseeing. Our first surprise on the trip was being given a fabulous suite at the Chateau when our regular room was not available. We had a living room, huge dining room, jacuzzi, plus regular bathroom, and bedroom suite, all furnished in spectacular antiques, with a view over Quebec and the river. It was almost difficult to leave the suite to explore old Quebec. One definite result of the new diagnosis was to loosen my thriftiness. I saw a hat I had to have, for instance, which, of course, I seldom ever wear. The trip ended at Niagara Falls, which we had never seen, and we explored the falls from every direction in Canada and the United States, too. The last night of our trip was quite stormy as one of the hurricanes that periodically hit the South attacked New York. But we made it to the Shaw Repertoire Theatre at Niagara on the Lake, where we enjoyed a comedy performance.

Two weeks before Memorial Day in 1986 we got a call from Tobae, with her husband, Russ, on the phone, too. "Mom, I have something to tell you," she started in a tremulous voice. What could be worse than to have your own daughter confronting breast cancer? She was devastated with fear. With two young children, her main concern was survival for them. Nothing I could say about all the improvements in therapy could allay her fears. I tried to get her to focus on the good prognosis, but for many months John and I could tell she thought of all the bad outcomes, with which, as a doctor, she was so much more aware than I had been.

She would hike and hike, almost possessed by hiking mania, between chemotherapies, to prove to herself that she had physical stamina. She lost her hair completely, but that did not seem to depress her as much as it would have me. She hated the feel of the wig in the summer months, and blithely walked around totally bald at home without seeming to agonize. After six months of sick leave, she returned to her office, wearing the wig to work, and gradually a soft fuzz on her head turned into short tight ringlets, as her hair came back.

As I babysat the boys while Tobae was in the hospital and then recuperating, I could sense their fear, too. The word "cancer" loomed as a scary monster. As Tobae's birthday approached, Daniel and Mark and I prepared to put on a show. Rap was much in vogue then, and Daniel, who was not prone to recitations or singing, was quite willing to write rap verses. I can remember the passion he put into his verses, all about how the "cancer was killed."

I think it helped them somewhat to act out their fears. I also remember that they had no trouble memorizing their verses, while I had to fall back on prompt notes to do my part. Daniel, who is sweet and thoughtful, could not resist prodding me, "Granny, when are you ever going to learn your lines?" To brighten Tobae's birthday, which came just a week or so after the mastectomy, Michael provided a real surprise. From Atlanta, he ordered a special Italian dinner delivered to her house from one of her favorite Everett restaurants. I remember that Russ and I, who were both in on the surprise, had to act as if we were feeling lazy to serve as a reason for not starting to cook dinner on time.

I believe the difference between Tobae's and my reaction to the diagnosis of cancer is explained partly by the difference in our stages in life: she had two young boys to whom she was everything a mother could be, while my children were grown, and no one was dependent on me. When anything appears in the news now about cancer, I focus on it not because of me, but solely because of Tobae. I anxiously waited for five years to pass, so that I could feel somewhat surer of her having overcome the episode. I really never thought that it might come back for me.

In the spring of 2008, however, I was feeling increasingly tired and out of breath. The pulmonologist advised respiratory therapy, which

I diligently pursued, only to feel worse and worse. John and my son Michael, my two doctors, were off on charter sailing off Belize, and not reachable by phone. My doctor hospitalized me, and the tests began. I was treated to every conceivable new technology, and by the time husband and son returned, the diagnosis came in— non-Hodgkin lymphoma. Fortunately it was the type of lymphoma most amenable to treatment.

We were allowed to proceed with the planned trip to the Georgia Municipal Convention in Savannah, followed by a short respite in Saint Simons at a nice resort. We had a lovely reunion with Carolyn and Don Carter, my dear friends from the 1940s when we were all starting our careers in Atlanta. Carolyn was the reporter who did a story on me in *Mademoiselle* when I worked in the labor movement, and back then Don was city editor of the *Atlanta Journal*. He progressed through the years to become the top executive of the Knight-Ridder newspaper chain.

It became obvious on our return drive to Atlanta that I was rapidly getting weaker with increasingly severe symptoms. Upon our return, my oncologist would hear of no postponement of the first chemotherapy treatment on June 30th and July 1st, the latter date coinciding with my eightieth birthday. We resolved to proceed with the long planned family reunion for the July 4th weekend, when all six grandchildren would converge upon us with all their energy and high spirits, together with parents and other assorted relatives. The big dinner was held at the local Westin hotel, where everyone was ensconced for the weekend. My memory of the weekend is that I participated in more or less of a zombie state, with everyone extremely solicitous and eager to help. I became aware of how grown up the grandchildren had become and objected to the amount of alcohol I observed them consume. They had a great time.

When the diagnosis came of lymphoma, I felt we had to go public. Obviously I would not be on all four burners for some months to come, and we could not keep it quiet. So Judy Parker, our consummate public relations director for the city of Sandy Springs, crafted a news release announcing my specific diagnosis and indicating I would continue my duties as mayor, with the help of the council and staff.

The day after the release I got a call from the *Atlanta Journal Constitution* reporter, questioning me about my cancer diagnosis. I corrected her indicating I had a much more specific diagnosis that I wished to have noted. My reticence reflects the scary effect the word "cancer" seems to have on the general public. After repeated conversations, involving also her supervisors, I was promised the paper would not use the word "cancer," but stick to my diagnosis of lymphoma. Imagine my anger the next day when the headline announced I had cancer, as well as the radio announcement on the station owned by the same corporation as the paper. To me this was a direct example of how newspapers tend to be sensational wherever possible.

This time with chemotherapy, I did lose all my hair. Somehow with tremendous help from John, Michael, and Michael's wife, Kelley, I got through the regime of chemo, including two blood transfusions when my red count went too low. Several times I lost my voice, which proved to be a great inconvenience in trying to conduct council meetings. Mayor Pro Tem Tibby DeJulio stepped in to help when I was reduced to a whisper. Everyone was most understanding; I missed not a single council session, and managed to keep up with daily duties. After six months the PET scan showed me to be in total remission, and it was time to retire another experience with cancer.

The Joy of Sailing

The first paycheck I earned in consulting was soon spent on a luxury. For many years, I had yearned to spend time on "THE Lake," as everyone referred to Lake Lanier. Johnny was being invited to spend weekends on the lake with his friend Bobby Warwick, whose father had constructed a motorboat in his garage. I felt we also needed a boat.

Without John, I took matters in hand and purchased an eighteen-foot, cat-rigged sailboat. I asked him to pay for the boat trailer. So began our sailing life. Neither of us knew anything about sailing, but John figured it could not be hard. All five of us crowded on this little boat and tried it out. As luck would have it, one of the early expeditions coincided with a summer thunderstorm. John found it was quite difficult to handle the boat, given his lack of knowledge. Luckily another boat came by and noticed our trouble. John was able to save the day with some advice, and nobody went overboard before we reached land. But it became obvious we needed instruction. The Coast Guard gave a course for beginning sailors, and we both took it and found it very helpful.

We made many excursions to the lake, exploring the coves and sharpening our sailing skills. One outing was unduly prolonged when we could not find where we had parked the car and trailer. Each cove at dusk looked just like the one where we knew we had launched, and yet again and again it turned out to be the wrong one. Finally, John beached the boat, and in his bathing suit flagged a ride, explaining, "I just can't seem to find my car. Would you mind giving me a ride to the next cove and see if it's there?" A worse episode involved the loss of the car keys overboard. Johnny was asked to hitchhike back to our home to retrieve the extra key and come back to the lake with the other car. For the next twenty years of sailing, we never had that same mishap again. I still carry my car key on a floater.

Our close friend Bill Eubanks developed an interest in sailing about this time, and we decided to buy a somewhat larger boat: an O'Day day sailor. For several years we shared that boat, but eventually sold it when Bill lost interest in sailing. John and I then graduated to a boat permanently moored to a dock (the Cal-20), which really simplified the preparation for getting started and finishing up. Although we later joined the Lake Lanier Sailing Club for a better anchorage and boat facilities, John never participated in the races sponsored by the club. Our pleasure was dealing with the wind and the ambiance of the water and scenery. To this day a picnic dinner on the boat at the end of a hot summer day is a treat to both of us during weekdays when the lake is empty. I still do not have the courage to handle the boat myself, but I have become a very competent crew. We are so synchronized now that there are no more frantic commands from the skipper of "get that boom loose!" or "steer into the wind, for God's sake, while I raise the main."

The sailing bug led John and me to chartering in the Caribbean. Twice we sailed out of the Virgin Islands with a Swiss couple, Rudi and Heidi Preisig. John had become acquainted with him at various liver meetings, and the four of us got along marvelously. We would move from anchorage to anchorage and relish languid cocktail hours watching the magnificent sunsets. We told jokes and funny stories, and acted like kids. Occasionally, instead of cooking in the galley, we would take the dinghy and motor to shore and enjoy marvelous fresh-fish dinners at one or another native restaurant. One evening, steering by flashlight, our dinghy became entangled in mooring lines of other anchored boats and then narrowly escaped marshy bottoms as we hit the shallows. What would seem sheer madness to us today was hilarious then.

I can remember Rudi and Heidi laughing with hysteria as I described our American system of credit cards. I went through my wallet itemizing what each of the twenty or so credit cards represented, and ended with the *piece de la resistance*: "And this is the credit card that insures all the other ones, if they get lost." Rudi countered, "Well, if you lose your wallet, won't that one be lost, too?"

Two seasons we were fortunate in luring the kids to sail with us. The first time, Tobae was suffering through her internship, and a week on the water was just what she needed. The boys were wonderful crew. The boat we chartered was a terrible old tub, and we were given insufficient instructions upon chartering. Nobody told us to check the oil level daily. So one afternoon we entered into a marina with smoke billowing from our engine, and the harbormaster made haste to help us tie up and turn off the engine. In our early experiences in the Virgin Islands, before we learned to become more careful about choosing a good charterer, we invariably had problems with the heads clogging up, which would mean radioing for service and then waiting endlessly at anchor for someone to respond.

The kids loved visiting one of the native restaurants and then staying for the dancing. Sidney's Peace and Love was an especially memorable destination. It consisted of a straw roof over some wooden-slat tables with picnic benches. Guests prepared their own drinks. The cost of the ice no doubt exceeded that of the rum in the drinks. For each drink, one made a mark next to one's boat name. (To our embarrassment, that year our boat was called "Chicken George." When our lobster dinner was ready, the call would come over the loudspeaker, "Chicken George, your dinners are ready.")

After dinner, the native help would dance with the tourists. The music was powered by a kerosene generator and lasted until midnight. The kids, of course, loved it, and insisted on staying to the end. We parents kept praying for the kerosene to give out, as the base and drums resonated over the water, no matter how far away we anchored.

The second family sailing expedition included Johnny and his new wife, Sylvia. They had been married only six months and hadn't really had a honeymoon. Poor Sylvia was deathly seasick, and I think relieved when she and Johnny finally disembarked to spend a few nights in a resort on their own. But she was a good sport. Johnny had learned to wind surf and showed his skill as he circulated around the anchorage.

An effort to get me on the board was fruitless. The only lasting result is a photo of my rear end, taken as I tried to mount the board.

Two of our major sailing expeditions entailed foreign travel: Tahiti and Turkey. Jim Keelin and Marilu McCarty were our partners on the Tahiti trip. Sailing within the lagoons was uneventful. Indeed, we were usually under engine. But reaching Bora Bora and other islands across the open Pacific required real sailing. Once, coming back from Bora Bora in a rainsquall, while seeking the entrance into the lagoon over the reefs to another island, Marilu and I were required to haul down the mainsail, with the boat rocking from side to side. It was all we could do to lower the sail and secure it to the boom, as we held on with one arm around the boom for dear life. Jim, who had served in the Navy in the Korean War, was the captain. He insisted on strict protocol and even required an accurate log be kept. That was the only job for which he felt I might be suited. The snorkeling in the lagoons was spectacular. We saw a wide variety of sea life including barracudas, sea cucumbers, eels, and so on. The sunsets as we anchored in the lagoon of Bora Bora were romantic and spectacular. We would postpone work in the galley until we had put the sun to bed over evening cocktails.

Our trip to Turkey in 1994 entailed a charter with a captain and cook. They were a delightful French couple that knocked themselves out to make the trip memorable. Sallie Newbill, my friend from Sandy Springs (and a state senator) was with us. Captain Philippe considered himself the great protector of the natives. He took us to visit the poorest of the poor in the hills around our anchorage. There we saw how the people subsisted on a few goats, living on a large platform covered with their Turkish rugs, with mosquito netting over all. This is where they slept and ate and where they served us tea. The unfortunate family was burdened with four daughters, a great problem since they were too poor to provide dowries. Philippe also knew where to find ancient ruins that were not even catalogued in the national registers. He would lead us into the hills and find remains of temples and habitations with Greek lettering. Most tourists see Ephesus, but fail to realize the whole country is full of ruins not yet explored or labeled.

Lucie was a fabulous cook. How, in the small galley, she managed to produce gourmet tortes and succulent roasts was more than I could fathom. One lunch was particularly memorable. We were anchored off some island, and Philippe had casually mentioned that this was really off limits to sailboats by decree of NATO (with which the Turkish Navy is affiliated.) As we lounged on deck with wine and appetizers, suddenly a Turkish Navy boat appeared, with sailors at the bow holding machine guns pointed in our direction.

The wine bottles were rapidly withdrawn below deck as we cleared the lunch. "We had engine trouble, and were just ready to cast off. We are Americans." The Turkish boat retreated and out came our lunch.

The Next Generation

Our children have done quite well for themselves. Tobae became a neurologist. She got a B.S. from Brown and M.D. at Emory and went into practice in Everett, Washington. Johnny went to Emory for a B.S. and the University of Illinois for a Ph.D. in nuclear engineering. He became chief scientist of the accelerator at Oak Ridge National Labs. Michael, meanwhile, followed in his Dad's footsteps. John trained him in gastroenterology, and he went into private practice at Piedmont. When John retired from Emory, he joined Michael in his practice and worked there until '85.

All our children married in the early 1980s, and each had two children. The arrival of the first grandchild was almost as thrilling as that of my own first child. I adored having the grandchildren with me when they were little. When siblings were born, I became the caretaker for the firstborn, to give the mothers some respite. John and I had a large role in teaching the little ones to put their faces in the water and to learn to swim. We read with the grandchildren snuggling up to see the pictures. I am keeping the best of the books we read in hopes that I can use them again with great-grandchildren.

Tobae is now the mother of two college graduates, one of whom just recently went to work for Facebook. Tobae is very apolitical. Her interests gravitate to skiing and hiking, and she has a ten-acre wonderland of blooming shrubs and trees that she has planted herself over the years. The older of Johnny's two kids is a Yale graduate and is now going to work at Google, and the younger is enrolling at Emory this fall. Johnny was always a very independent fellow, wanting to do it all by himself, and his son has the same disposition. My grandson was a speaker at his high school graduation, for example, and his parents did not even know he would be speaking until he got up on the podium to begin. Michael's two kids are University of Georgia students.

We visit the Seattle area once a year, and my daughter comes east in the fall. We see the Oak Ridge folks three or four times a year, and, of course, we see the Atlanta set quite often.

The six grandchildren are close in age (now from age eighteen to twenty-two) and have become close buddies despite the distances. When they were young we arranged common vacations for all the families, and so the cousins became close from the time in diapers to later reunions as college students. One of our best vacations was take all the children and grandchildren heli-hiking in British Columbia. The closeness they established will last these cousins a lifetime, I hope.

Part Two
ONE LONG DAY AT A TIME:
Making the Dream Called
The City of Sandy Springs
Come True

"Eva!" The First Campaign

Exposure to the zoning battles, and the lack of responsiveness of the County Commission to Sandy Springs' issues propelled me into politics. In 1965 I ran my first race as a Democrat for the Georgia General Assembly. I was a total novice, naive to say the least, and thought all I had to do was tell people about my qualifications, and I'd get the votes. The seat went to someone I considered not properly qualified, and I should have learned my lesson.

I continued my involvement in the community, especially as Atlanta made efforts to annex Sandy Springs. By 1976 I was convinced that local control, with a city of our own, was the only answer for Sandy Springs. The sentiment in Sandy Springs against annexation was almost unanimous. A big rally was held on the subject in a high school auditorium, and I rose to speak and minced no words. "Let's call a spade a spade," I spoke. "The only reason they want to annex us is for our tax base." Mayor Jackson, who was a black man, led Atlanta by then. I heard a titter through the audience, and couldn't figure out what was so funny about my comments. When I got home I related the incident to the family, and the kids exploded in laughter. "Mom, don't you know what a 'spade' refers to? You just don't watch enough television to know the modern lingo." I was crestfallen, and terribly embarrassed, especially since my comments were reported in the newspaper the next day, with my picture across four columns of the paper.

Luckily the SREB, for which I was working then, was holding its annual meeting out of town, so I figured my bosses would not have seen the article. No such luck. The Atlanta paper reporters covering the meeting made sure my bosses saw the article.

I made haste to personally apologize to the black senator who was seated on the dais the night of the hearing. I think he understood I really had not known the other interpretation of that word, and he was gracious.

By 1978, the state representative of my district was giving up the seat to attend Harvard Business School, and I jumped into the race for the Republican nomination to capture his seat. By that time I was firmly converted to a more conservative outlook, and the district was definitely a Republican one. It included both Roswell and half of Sandy Springs. I was pretty well known in Sandy Springs as a result of my zoning and planning activities, but had no base whatsoever in Roswell, which comprised more than half of the district.

Connie Russell volunteered to serve as my campaign chairman. I figured she would know what to do, since she had worked in the successful campaign of a Republican congressman. But, alas, that is not quite as things worked out. Connie was fabulous about helping with the campaign "literature." A brochure was developed, yard signs were ordered, and bumper stickers produced, with only one word: "EVA!"

What Connie failed to emphasize, or I didn't hear from her, was the futility of visiting door to door and meeting hundreds of people who were possibly non-registered, or even Democrats. I went neighborhood-to-neighborhood, ringing doorbells. I wore out shoes, lost unwanted pounds, and saw every type of architecture and landscaping as I covered the territory. When nobody answered the door, I could leave my brochure in the mailbox, with a sorry-I-missed-you note. Saturday after Saturday I followed the routine.

My primary opponent, Luther Colbert, was savvy. He had the printout of the Republicans who had voted in the last primary, and he drove only to their addresses. His was a much more economical effort since the election would be determined in the Republican primary. Although in later years Luther and I became good friends, during a campaign it's always "dog-eat-dog," and he painted me as a raging liberal after dredging up that I had worked for the *Journal of Labor*. When we appeared at meetings together, he infuriated me by insisting on referring to "Dr. Galambos." I thought he was making fun of a pinheaded intellectual. I found out in later years that he sincerely admired education, to the extent that as a legislator he enrolled in a baccalaureate program to complete a degree later in life. In fact, he died in an automobile accident one evening while driving home from one of his college courses.

One of the most frustrating elements of a local legislative race is to place yard signs advertising one's candidacy. Each of these signs must be laboriously erected in the front yards of supporters. We commandeered our children to help put the signs out, and it became quite tiresome to have to replace them in the hard dirt after a sizzling dry spell. We felt sure the other side was pulling our signs, and accused them of doing so. Eventually one of our folks caught a guy who had pulled them and who was duly reported to the justice of the peace, who happened to be a supporter. When the man was arraigned, it turned out he wasn't involved in the campaign at all. He had a girlfriend with my name, and kept regaling her with my "EVA!" signs.

The most memorable event of the campaign took place the eve of the primary. Connie called about eleven at night, and announced, "Eva, we've got to check on our mailbox stuffings. I'm sure they are taking our literature out." How she sensed the impending "crime," I never learned. Maybe it was part of the usual *modus operandi*. At any rate, with unerring instinct she headed to a neighborhood off Spalding Drive and started checking the mailboxes, which had earlier been stuffed by our supporters. Sure enough, they contained Luther's literature, while ours had been removed! That led to a wild escapade of emptying their stuff and putting ours back. The car filled up with what we had taken out, and we pushed it under the seat and anywhere we could hide it. Occasionally we would err and take out actual mail. That led to a wild effort to backtrack our route and to reinsert the real mail in the appropriate mailbox.

Finally at around two in the morning we crossed the opponent's path. There was a fairly loud confrontation in the middle of a quiet residential street with Luther's supporter, who turned out to be a Roswell City council member. "We'll stop pulling your stuff, if you'll leave ours alone." By the wee hours of the morning the whole situation seemed incredulously ludicrous. I arrived home and had a snack, falling into bed after gales of laughter. "Is this what campaigns are really about?" I thought. On election day, I decided to wash windows. It seemed to be the most sensible way to spend the time. That evening one of our supporters called the results in from downtown where the ballots were being tabulated. I had come in second in the three-man race, with a run-off in three weeks. But by then Connie and I knew that the Roswell contingent was more numerous than Sandy Springs', and that Luther would win. That's how it came out, too.

Saving Our Springs

In the 1960s the downtown Atlanta leadership was hell bent on expanding Atlanta's city limits to the north, which meant into Sandy Springs. A group was formed at that time, S.O.S., for "Save Our Springs," which vocalized the fervent opposition in the area to any annexation into the City of Atlanta. State law at that time permitted annexation by local statute, without any input by referendum of affected citizens. An annexation bill made its way through the Georgia House of Representatives against the furor from the unincorporated area, only to be stopped at the last minute when the Lieutenant Governor Lester Maddox, who presided in the Georgia Senate, locked the bill in his desk drawer so it could not be passed.

As the threat of annexation repeatedly surfaced into the seventies, it became clear to me that our stance in Sandy Springs should be a positive one: create our own city instead of opposing annexation. By that time I had suffered sufficient exposure to the Fulton County government, especially its wanton over-development of our community, to be convinced that the solution lay in forming our own city and controlling our own zoning.

In the seventies, the Sandy Springs business community looked on the formation of a City of Sandy Springs as a crazy notion, and the support came solely from the residents. Governor Busbee appointed a Study Commission chaired by the respected Judge Sidney Smith, to determine what to do about the conflicting desires of Atlanta and the suburbs. The Study Commission held hearings, and a particularly memorable one was held in Sandy Springs. Two of our supporters, Louis Holliman and Frank Gordy, donned Indian feathers and dumped tea before the astounded members of the group. The Committee for Sandy Springs monopolized the podium that night, pushing and pushing a City of Sandy Springs as a different solution than the Study Commission was contemplating—annexation of or consolidation of Sandy Springs and Atlanta. In preparation we had secured some 7,000 signatures from the community, requesting that we be allowed to vote on our own city.

One of the charges to the Study Commission was to recommend an equitable system of financing local services in the unincorporated area. We testified that we had no objection to paying for services we received (then financed by countywide taxes to which Atlantans contributed) if we could control how those funds were spent. In other words, give us the right to form a city and we'll be glad to pay for our services. It all boiled down to taxation with representation.

The outcome of this exercise was creation of the Special Tax District, which levies a special tax on the unincorporated area to pay for its local services. From an economist's perspective I could not argue with this outcome. From a citizen's viewpoint, however, I joined the ensuing furor that we were being taxed without representation.

After this defeat the Committee for Sandy Springs went into hibernation. I ran for the Legislature in 1978 with my major issue continuing to be a City of Sandy Springs, but, of course, lost the election. The time just wasn't right to pursue the issue. By 1988, however, the consternation in the community was at a crescendo, and I reactivated the Committee for Sandy Springs. We called an open meeting in the fall to restart the effort and were overwhelmed by the standing-room-only attendance in the parlor of the Hitson Memorial Center.

The first move was to arrange for a petition drive at the polls of the presidential election in November 1988. We deployed volunteers at each precinct to man the petition table. Voters were asked to sign a petition that sought a referendum on local government in Sandy Springs.

Soon we learned of a law that prohibits petition drives within 250 feet of a polling place. This location would in many cases have put us in the backyards of adjacent homes, or across the street of major arteries.

Plus, we thought, this was an infringement of our freedom of speech. We were not petitioning about anything on the ballot. We were just, rather, exercising our rights as American citizens.

I had visions of being hauled off to jail if we did not secure a court order enjoining the state from enforcing the 250-foot distance. Jim Anderson, a young Sandy Springs attorney, volunteered to represent us in the United States District Court before Judge O'Kelly. Jim did a wonderful job and seemed pleased to plead his first United States Constitutional case in our behalf. The judge issued the injunction, and we were free to obtain the signatures without fear of imprisonment. We secured some 20,000 signatures in one day. The petition pages were eventually attached to one another and then rolled into a huge scroll. In later years we took the scroll to legislative hearings and unrolled it down the middle of hearing rooms with great flourish. Incidentally, the law was eventually amended to 150 feet from the polling place and now specifically prohibits any kind of petitions within that distance.

So in 1989, fortified with our victories, we sought passage of a bill to hold a referendum in Sandy Springs. This was the beginning of a torturous process, played out year after year, in which we were always defeated. The House of Representatives has a "local courtesy" procedure whereby bills that deal with local matters within a county (such as incorporation of a new city) must secure assent within the local delegation for that county. The Fulton delegation at that time had eighteen members, of whom only five represented the North Fulton area. Moreover, the delegation had a rule that a measure must secure two-thirds of the total delegates to pass. We could never pass that threshold with the City of Atlanta dead set against a City of Sandy Springs. Twice we passed the bill in the senate, only to see it die in the house.

One year our state senator, Sallie Newbill, got really creative. She drew up a bill that would annex Sandy Springs to a chartered, but non-activated, city across the river in Cobb County—Chattahoochee Plantation. Since the bill dealt with two counties, we reasoned that the local courtesy problem would not catch it. We were wrong. The Speaker of the Georgia House at the time was Tom Murphy. As the speaker,

Murphy had absolute control over the house, and he ruled the bill to be a local bill, and it died in the Fulton delegation. (Many of us had played around with possible names for this city while the prospect was still alive—Sandyhoochee, or Chattasprings.)

With prospects so dim in the legislature, we tried the judicial route. We raised funds at a gala ball and auction and hired attorneys. Yet three different attorneys and their efforts led nowhere. They were never able to hit upon the right precedents of attack to challenge the shenanigans of the Georgia House.

By 1994 our state representative, Dorothy Felton, came up with a novel idea: why not seek passage of a general law that applies statewide to circumvent the local-courtesy barrier? She had a bill drawn that tightly constrained the conditions when new cities could be formed via referendum. It was so tightly drawn that it only applied in four counties besides ours. It made it through committee, and onto the floor of the House. We had lobbied for many days to secure assent by a majority of the 180 representatives in the House. During the summer months we had even organized visits throughout the state, assigning different legislators to various members of the committee. One of those I landed on my list had his lumber business off in the hinterland of South Georgia. He was so astounded to be visited by two ladies from Sandy Springs that he almost committed to vote for our bill. During the legislative sessions, I darted from one legislator's office to another's morning after morning, trying to catch my prey and to convert him or her to our cause. (The whole process of standing in the hallways trying to waylay legislators is a demeaning one that I never enjoyed.)

The morning of our vote in 1994, the speaker sent out word to his committee chairmen not to vote for the bill. Many were individuals who had committed to us. When the bill came up for a vote, it lost by three votes. Had the men's restroom not been full of the legislators with their marching orders, it would have passed. We suffered utter despair.

Yet, having come so close, we felt we had to try again. We organized letter-writing campaigns to legislators statewide. If a Sandy Springs supporter had a friend of relative in another county, we asked him or her to write to that person to promote letter writing by constituents to their delegates. By 1995, however, the speaker realized that if we got our bill to the floor of the house, it would pass. Therefore it was repeatedly delayed in committee, so that it would have to be bottled up in the rules committee, which the speaker controls and which never let the bill out.

Our only success came in 1996 when the chairman of the state planning and urban affairs committee secured passage for us of legislation that now requires a referendum when any annexation is to take place. No longer may the state legislature pass a bill that mandates annexation of an area without a referendum.

So, after annual attempts to pass both the local and the general bill, it was still a standoff between Atlanta and Sandy Springs. Atlanta couldn't annex us, and yet the central city continued to stymie our efforts in the legislature. In 1998 we had hoped to elect a majority Republican house of representatives, but this was a daydream that did not happen. Indeed, the turnout was so great in the election (and almost totally for Democrats) that the other side could claim the statewide Democratic sweep was due to their efforts. The Republican candidate for lieutenant governor, who lived in Sandy Springs, unfortunately let the race degenerate into a campaign that relied heavily on racial implications. That seemed to activate a particularly heavy voter turnout among black people, while many white voters were disgusted by the negative campaign. The black caucus in the Georgia house then held its contribution to the Democrat victory over the heads of the white Democrat leadership. Indeed, sadly enough, the entire Sandy Springs issue in the legislature had degenerated into a black-white one. It was almost a mark of honor on the part of the black legislators to hold a veto power over Sandy Springs. Moreover, the leadership of the Georgia House was dependent on the black vote to stay in power. It was an unholy alliance that we were not able to break, despite growing unrest, editorial support, and unanimity within the Sandy Springs community. Individually, the Democratic representatives from across the state commiserated and sympathized with our plight. When the speaker put out the word, however, they followed orders.

Countless hours had been spent in fruitless negotiations with

Atlanta officials and representatives to try to find a compromise. These negotiations went nowhere; they were not meant to succeed. Their purpose was always to delay until the session of the General Assembly expired. In 1999 we offered to allow Atlanta to annex the Powers Ferry Landing area, which contained prime commercial property and high-rise office towers. Not a single resident was included in an area, which would generate four million dollars annually in taxes to Atlanta. Yet Atlanta turned this down, claiming that it would cost the City of Atlanta financially to annex the area. When we inquired how a totally prime commercial area could cost rather than create net revenues, we were told it would entail having to build another fire station. It seemed like total poppycock to us, since the area had no county station then, and nobody seemed to feel it was unprotected. Moreover, all kinds of reciprocal arrangements could be worked out between fire departments. The city response seemed trumped up to us, and indicative once again of the fact that negotiations seemed to be fruitless.

Through the years the quest for cityhood became a personal mission for me. I was totally involved emotionally. This had its positives as well as negatives. Since retirement, it served as an outlet for my energies, and I certainly enjoyed the many contacts with the community resulting from my growing notoriety. I enjoyed speaking engagements, especially the question-and-answer periods when I interacted with the audience. The support for incorporation in Sandy Springs had deepened and matured through the years.

Even the tediousness of keeping up a computerized database that included up to 1,800 families, with current updates on their financial contributions, was less a chore and more a pleasurable part of tending to "my group." Indeed, the chores having to do with the Committee for Sandy Springs motivated my gradual acquaintance with more and more computer applications. Increasingly, we were moving to an automated electronic communication system as more and more folks had email.

Yet the emotional blows as we were defeated year after year did take their toll. I hung on to every shred of possible good news as the legislative session ground on, in the slim hope that something would be salvaged, knowing deep down it wouldn't happen. Sometimes the frustration got so heavy that I was tempted to go in the middle of the night with a spray paint can to cover up the "un" in the "unincorporated" designation for the signs that announced entrance into the Sandy Springs community.

I recall the defeat on the floor of the House in 1994 as especially traumatic. To have come so close! I was scheduled the next day for arbitration in Tennessee and consciously used the trip for catharsis. I stopped to shop in a discount mall on the way as a total distraction, something I normally would not do. Then I looked forward to a good visit with Johnny and his family in Oak Ridge.

Sandy Springs—Yes!

Our quest for an incorporated Sandy Springs continued, with the new state representative, Joe Wilkinson, who tried desperately to help us, including direct meetings with Speaker Murphy. He reported to me about one such meeting with my nemesis. Speaker Murphy did recall that my father had taught him in law school at the University of Georgia. But so unlike all Dad's former students, the speaker had only an unkind remark to make: "I remember I couldn't understand his lectures because of his German accent."

We went to extremes in trying to gain the support of the Fulton delegation. I remember one meeting with Senator Vincent Fort, a black leader who had always opposed us. One of the younger Committee for Sandy Springs Board members was convinced that if we just approached our opponents on a human scale, and pled our case, they would listen. So we arranged a meeting with Fort. He kept us waiting for forty-five minutes past our appointed time, and to this day I am convinced it was for effect. We had even brought home-baked cookies, in our earnest and misguided belief that we could reason with the gentleman.

I had made similar efforts with Representative Tyrone Brooks, a civil rights leader serving in the Fulton delegation. One of Brooks' accomplishments had been a successful restoration of a city charter to a group of black citizens who wanted to resurrect a moribund charter for Lizella, Georgia. I appealed to his sense of justice that we should be accorded the same rights to self-government, but made no progress.

As we raised our demands over the years, the reception by the black members of the Fulton County Commission to our quest for local government became more and more hostile. At one commission meeting, Commissioner Nancy Boxill at one Commission said, "Why doesn't Sandy Springs just move lock stock and barrel to Chattanooga!"

It was always evident that nobody in Sandy Springs would be interested in forming our own city if to do so would increase taxes. So it was important from day one of persuading folks to get on board to have data to prove the taxes would not go up. A lot of us knew intuitively that we were paying more taxes into the Special Tax District (which was supposed to pay for our local services like police, fire, recreation, planning and zoning and some limited public works) than we were getting in services delivered by Fulton County. It was important to document this conclusion.

The work I had done as a consultant in various Georgia jurisdictions on double taxation entailed exactly the same methodology needed to analyze the Sandy Springs fiscal picture. So I tackled it. My early attempts were fairly unsophisticated. As the years went by, however, and freedom-of-information legislation guaranteed more and more access to citizens, it became easier to get real data. Repeated studies showed wider and wider discrepancies between the taxes Sandy Springs paid, and the services it received from the county. We analyzed the Special Tax District separately from the General Fund. The latter is the big countywide fund that pays for countywide services like the justice system, the jail, libraries, Grady Hospital, and human and social services. It turned out that Sandy Springs was paying about nine times more into the fund than it was deriving by virtue of services financed by the General Fund. However, we took great pains throughout the years to always stress that we were not complaining about this imbalance. Sandy Springs as a higher income community was bound to bear a disproportionate burden for income redistributive services like Grady Hospital, which serves the indigent. We were not fussing about paying our share for that. We were indignant, on the other hand, as we learned through the years how much of our Special Tax District fund was being spent elsewhere, totally out of proportion to what other areas contributed in taxes.

Eventually the county administration determined that it needed to conduct its own analysis of the skew for the Special Tax District fund. The amazing result showed an even greater exodus of our money to South Fulton County than we had calculated. To make sure the numbers were right, Tibby De Julio and I met with the budget director of Fulton County. He ended up by telling us he had advised the county manager not to divulge the results of the study, because, as he said, "It will make them even madder!" The irony is that this gentleman, happily for us, became the first finance director of the new city of Sandy Springs.

In the end the discrepancy turned into a redistribution of our tax money to South Fulton County in the amount of fifty cents out of our every one of our tax dollars into the Special Tax District. We fumed and circulated the data. We didn't mind shouldering our portion of the burden for Grady Hospital, but we did want to keep our tax dollars for police and fire at home. We were tired of being used as a cash cow.

Obviously the receiving end of our subsidy fought like tigers to try to keep it. The dispute degenerated into a series of competing flyers, web messages, and political speeches, but there was no way to paper over the truth. Eventually South Fulton lost our subsidy, and its taxes for local services had to be raised. The county commissioners representing that area engaged in spirited retribution. During the referendum on the City of Sandy Springs the South Fulton commissioners were still hurling accusations at the Sandy Springs incorporation move. In the community, our folks felt every blast from South Fulton increased the positive support for the City of Sandy Springs by another 1,000 votes.

Another big fiscal issue that kept rearing its head during the many years of negotiations for the right to hold the referendum on the City of Sandy Springs entailed the local option sales tax. Fulton County levies a countywide one-percent sales tax to help the operation of local governments. The take is divided by a formula negotiated by the county and the mayors of the cities within the county after each census. Obviously, creation of another city would mean some jurisdiction would lose sales tax when a new city like Sandy Springs became eligible for its share of the pie. We in Sandy Springs felt the need to soften the impact on the city of Atlanta with regards to the sales tax, and we turned ourselves into pretzels trying to figure out formulas that would soften the blow to Atlanta, and yet eventually gain the rightful share for Sandy Springs. The news that we were offering to split our share of the sales tax was not well received in Sandy Springs. So there was always the tension of trying to get a bill that would fly versus giving away funds that would be needed to run the new city.

Calculations on the sales tax split occupied me for years and did not lead to agreement by the Fulton delegation. However, the General Assembly as a whole understood ever more clearly that we were not going away, and that we would be there year after year pushing our cause.

By January 2003, the largest Sandy Springs legislative district gained new leadership as Representative Dorothy Felton retired after many years of pushing our bills unsuccessfully. Representative Joe Wilkinson knocked himself out from day one to make friends with everyone in the Georgia House, and he had the outgoing, gregarious personality to make inroads. So in 2004, during the second year of his first term, we pushed especially hard. By then a new Democratic Speaker ruled the Georgia House of Representatives, and we hoped to have better luck. Again, we lobbied and worked on individual legislators, seeking them out again on their home grounds.

Tibby deJulio and I decided during this time to visit Congressman John L. Lewis, who is revered by the black community for his brave participation in the Selma, Alabama, civil-rights march. He had been beaten in the head at that time as the younger black generation was insisting on its rightful role in society. He is a civil rights hero. He espoused the right to vote for everyone, black or white. Would he endorse our right to a referendum on cityhood?

To our delight Congressman Lewis did not hesitate and promised to attend the annual meeting of the Committee for Sandy Springs. Tibby and I felt we were dancing on a cloud as we exited the downtown building housing Lewis' offices. Not only did he attend, but he also gave a ringing endorsement of our right to vote. There was emotional dynamite when Congressman Lewis said to the standing-room-only congregation of Sandy Springs citizens in the social hall of the Sandy Springs United Methodist Church, "I fought for the right of black folks to vote, and so I have to support this same right for you and for all citizens." The assemblage rose to its feet with thunderous applause. The sense of good feeling that permeated the group was palpable. The Congressman was echoing our message, and for the first time a black leader had the courage to speak of our rights, too.

We taped the speech and bought a portable DVD player so we could take the speech downtown to the legislative session and play it for the legislators. We were amazed when some of the black local leadership brushed off Lewis' endorsement of our cause as meddling in local affairs.

Throughout the years there was the quest for finding a deal whereby the Sandy Springs bill could be swapped for something the other side wanted passed. A particularly good opportunity gave us hope in 2004: the City of Atlanta needed the support of our Republican delegates in the Georgia House to pass legislation for an 8th cent of sales tax to bail the city out of its sewer crisis. The deal we pursued and thought we had in hand entailed a swap by our folks for the 8th cent in return for allowing the referendum bill to move out. The bill had passed in the Senate, and we needed it passed in the House. In the waning moments of the session the deal came apart. The vote for the 8th cent went forward, and ours died.

During our years in the legislative wilderness, we were busily planning the structure of our city. We appointed a Charter Commission, which met for a year designing the charter for the new city. One of the most contentious issues was the matter of the council and mayoral salaries. The predominant opinion was that we wanted citizens to run for office who were interested in public service, not for the pay. We set ridiculously low salaries at $15,000 for the mayor and $7,500 for the council members. The legislators changed these provisions to $25,000 for the mayor and $12,500 for the council members.

One of the most important messages we pressed home over and over again in the referendum campaign was that with the new city, property taxes would stay the same. This was extremely important, because few folks were so eager for their own local government that they would pay more taxes to achieve the goal. We had taken great pains to include in the charter for the city, which was part of the legislation for the referendum, that the tax rate for the new city could not exceed 4.731 million, then the existing tax rate Fulton County was levying for the special tax district. Since the special tax district would go away with the new city, there would be no tax increase.

We decided this was a time to go for business support, in addition to many smaller contributions from residents. With a tight schedule, we raised more than enough funds to pay for the campaign. We also staged a barbecue featuring Governor Perdue, a sold-out affair.

The Charter Commission also discussed the desirability of having some Council members run at large, if not all of them. But in the end the strong desire for local representation overcame this strategy; the charter made every council member represent a separate geographic area.

The battle was finally won when the Republican party took over the majority of the Georgia House of Representatives in the November 2004 election. As the number of winners on our side edged over the magic number of 91, and on into the 100s, we knew our time was coming. Now Georgia had a Republican senate, house and governor. Our quest was finally becoming totally real. Immediately the push was on to pass our referendum bill. Suddenly the rules changed, and the waters parted. Hearings were held, including one standing-room-only event in Sandy Springs that attracted so many folks the police had to close the road.

Oliver Porter had rejoined the Board of Directors of the Committee for Sandy Springs by this time, and he badgered us at every meeting to transcend the euphoria and to focus on how we would run a city, given we would probably pass the bill in the 2005 session. Meeting after meeting he brought flow charts and designs for task forces, nudging us toward the serious work of establishing a new city. We named him interim city manager (without salary), and he guided the organizational efforts to its successful conclusion. His own volume on his effort, *Creating the City of Sandy Springs*, tells the story in its entirety.

A wrinkle was injected into the legislative process when a legislator from North Fulton County north of our boundaries added an amendment to the effect that a small island within the described new city limits would be carved out. This produced a huge hullabaloo in the affected neighborhood—one with the most expensive real estate in all of Sandy Springs. The vast majority of the neighbors wanted into the new city limits, and a small contingent wanted out. The leader of the "leave us out" group was Bert Levy, a lawyer with a major firm downtown. When questioned at a public meeting why he wanted out, he replied that he did not want to be part of Atlanta, nor Sandy Springs, but just to remain an unincorporated island. It turned out that his rationale was that he could obtain a higher real estate appraisal of his home if it were listed as "Buckhead," the most prestigious district in metro Atlanta.

All hell broke loose in this neighborhood, which mobilized itself full strength. Surveys were put in the mailboxes of every home in the affected Northside neighborhood, with a query as to whether they wanted to be in the City of Sandy Springs, remain unincorporated, or go into Atlanta.

The response was overwhelming. First of all, the response rate was amazing—over 50% to a mailbox stuffing. The results were more than 80% in favor of the City of Sandy Springs. With this information, the legislator was forced to retreat and take his amendment off the bill. I had a little fun with this whole episode because I had a copy of the letter from Mr. Levy to Senator Isakson stating his desire to stay out of Sandy Springs. It was written on the letterhead of the law firm. I did write the law firm's managing partner to inquire whether this was a position of the law firm. I believe a Monday-morning meeting in their offices dealt with the issue.

The bill in 2005 was handled as a general one, which did not need the endorsement of the Fulton delegation. It sailed through the designated committees of both chambers of the Georgia General Assembly and ended on the floor of both houses for a lively debate. The Atlanta delegates fought us to the last, but we prevailed by healthy margins. I was in the galleries of both chambers when the bill passed and felt unbelievable happiness both times. The next day the daily paper featured me with my arms raised in glee as the vote totals registered on the official electronic voting panel.

The legislation to authorize the referendum passed in March 2005. The referendum for the folks in Sandy Springs to have their say was set for June twenty-first. Fortunately two of the Board members of the Committee for Sandy Springs were political campaign pros, with one, Rusty Paul, owner of a public relations firm. Rusty and Gabriel Sterling were put in charge of the referendum, while Tibby and I raised funds to pay for the campaign.

A public relations campaign was mounted, completed with brochures that sought to answer all the major issues. Speakers fanned out throughout the community to spread the message, mostly to neighborhood associations and to service clubs. Yard signs proclaiming, "YES! SANDY SPRINGS" blossomed throughout neighborhood front yards.

The night of the returns was a moment of absolute jubilation. With scouts assigned to the various precincts we had calls coming in as the votes were tallied. When the first came in with over ninety per cent support we could hardly believe it. Then precinct after precinct came in with the same high scores. In the end we won the vote with a ninety-four per cent approval rating. I finally realized my longtime dream of removing the "un" from "Unincorporated Sandy Springs." Rusty Paul had come up with a banner where we peeled off the irritating "UN" and proclaimed our victory in our downtown park. The crowds went wild.

Forming a City Government

There was no time for continuing celebrations. We faced the start-up of our city just five months away. The Charter (for technical reasons) specified a start date of December 1, 2005. How were we to start a city from scratch, for 90,000 people, in five months?

That's when Oliver Porter's advance preparations really bore fruit. Immediately, he organized task forces on every facet of city government to be staffed by volunteers with suitable skills and backgrounds. We had a task force for every conceivable function of city government, from information technology to police and fire departments. The community enthusiastically went to work developing guidelines and directions and demonstrated a tremendous spirit of civic involvement. It was a sign of things to come when the city actually became functional. The contributions of these task forces in some areas were astounding. The one that dealt with the police department, for example, actually itemized the equipment that would be needed and estimated its costs.

More importantly, Porter had directed the attention of the Committee for Sandy Springs to the example of a new city in Florida: Weston. A private firm was running the city, with the exception of public-safety services, which were provided by the county. With all of us attuned to benefits of the private sector, we were anxious to learn more about it, even before the referendum. The more we heard about this approach, the more it appealed to us. We were philosophically attuned to outsourcing government, and we were under a terrible time pressure to gear up a government with a myriad of different services. This necessity also led in the direction of the private sector.

The details of how Oliver Porter was able to address the selection of a private firm to provide city services are described in his book. Suffice it to say it was a miracle. International corporations that might be interested were identified, and eventually responses by bidders were evaluated, all under the cover and guidance of the Governor's Commission, which lent respectability to the whole process. Amazingly by late fall one firm had been selected: Ch2MHill OMI. It undertook the start-up on a handshake. There was no city government in place when they started, so no city official could sign any papers, and the Governor's Commission was an oversight group with no power to sign contracts. So the city began on the basis of mutual faith between the corporation and Oliver Porter. And it worked, despite lawyers offering reams of advice on the side. Coverage of the company's start-up costs was included in the amount for the first year's contract, which exceeded the cost for the second year.

Under the contract Ch2MHill provides every service of the new City of Sandy Springs except police and fire and emergency response. The company handles all public works, planning and zoning, parks and recreation, and the various administrative functions (accounting, human relations, communications, information technology, and purchasing). The City Manager does not have the right to hire and fire any of the Ch2MHill employees, but is consulted on personnel matters. Yet he manages the affairs of the various departments. It is an arrangement that requires diplomacy and yet firmness, and a degree of mutual trust between the parties. For us, it works.

Our most concrete sign that outsourcing works is that we have fewer employees (counting both the firm's and ours) than our immediately neighboring city of similar size. We attribute the result to the much greater flexibility, which the private firm has to adjust to needed staffing, as well as to greater satisfaction of the employees as members of a vast firm, which offers them a multitude of new career paths. The shift of personnel to areas of greater need, as less is needed in other sections, is painless. The amount of turnover has been remarkably low. If new needs arise, or some recede, change orders are negotiated between the parties. The contract is renewable annually and must be rebid after five years.

Some changes have been made under the contract between the parties as experience was gained with the new arrangement. The finance director was originally a Ch2MHill employee. There was mutual agreement this would not work. So he is now a City of Sandy Springs employee. The firm somehow never got the human resources department to work properly. A huge portion of its workload relates to the police and fire employees, who are city employees. So the decision was reached to solicit new bids from the private sector for this service.

After years of distress with Fulton County's 911 service, including recurrent dispatch delays, the decision was made for the City of Sandy Springs (in partnership with another new city, Johns Creek) to start our own 911 service. This, too, was bid out, to be performed by a private contractor.

I ran for mayor in the November 8th election. My opponent came out of the woodwork, so to speak. Although he was a descendant of a large, well-known original family of Sandy Springs and Dunwoody (Spruill or Spruell, depending on the spelling of various branches), he was totally unknown in the community. Since I had been promoting the City of Sandy Springs for months at countless community gatherings, there really was not another big grass roots campaign. We had mailings and yard signs and a few major speaking events.

The election was officially non-partisan, but it was generally known I was a member of the Republican party (as was true of almost all the eventual council candidates.) The Democrats were backing Tim Spruell against me. He made a valiant effort. I won with eighty-nine per cent of the vote.

My family was very dubious about my political activities and my quest to establish the City of Sandy Spring. The kids were not enthusiastic about putting out yard signs when I ran for office for the first time. My family did not think the city would ever happen. However, after it did, they all rallied around and think it is a great outcome. The grandchildren had a grand time taking a photo with me behind my desk at city hall.

A major decision had to be made on where city hall would be located. Naturally it would have to be leased space, since our yet-to-be-born city had absolutely no funds. One of the Committee for Sandy Springs Board members was a commercial real estate broker and the logical choice to assist in the search for space. The choices narrowed down to renting in a high rise in the vicinity of Georgia 400 (where the high rises are concentrated) or a one-story building on Roswell Road, half a mile beyond the building, which had served as government headquarters for the Fulton County functions in Sandy Springs. I liked the campus feeling of the low-rise building, where we eventually signed a lease for an entire u-shaped building, which accommodates every department except public safety quite comfortably. There is nothing luxurious about it, but it meets the needs. The court space becomes the council chamber and is headquarters for other city commissions and boards when they meet.

Coincidentally the city hall is only one mile from my house, which is obviously a big plus, since I like conducting day-in and day-out business from my home office, but can hop over to city hall on short notice. While I might be accused of choosing a space to suit my convenience, everyone agrees in retrospect that the traffic congestion in the alternate high-rise locations was a terrible disadvantage and was to be avoided if possible.

As with everything connected with the start-up before the city existed, Ch2MHill was indispensable. We could not have signed any lease papers until December first, and we needed build-out immediately. Ch2MHill stepped into the breach.

The official start-up of the City of Sandy Springs occurred the night of November 30, 2005. (The first council session was held at 12:00 a.m. on December 1st.) Representative Joe Wilkinson (who had worked in his early career with President Reagan and White House ceremonies) was in charge of the inaugural, which proceeded with pomp and circumstance. Our makeshift city hall was duly decorated with blue and silver balloons. Elegant cloth hangings camouflaged the makeshift dais, and a local cadre of Revolutionary War re-enactors in full regalia performed the full color ceremonies. Supreme Court of Georgia Judge Heinstein administered a rather long oath of office. Acceptance speeches were delivered. The residents of Sandy Springs hugged each other in joy: Their dream had come true.

Eva receives the key to the City from Oliver Porter,
Inauguration 2005

Afterword for Part Two:
A New City Underway

One of my earliest soul-searching quandaries was whom to choose as city attorney. That position requires a person with whom the mayor works closely. There has to be rapport and trust. I agonized for weeks. I felt a debt to both the potential candidates and pressed for some way they could form a partnership, which would relieve me of playing Solomon. There was no other issue early on that gave me more sleepless nights or more seemingly endless discussions with John. Eventually, I went with the choice that made me comfortable—Wendell Willard, and I have never regretted it.

The initial meetings of the city council were largely guided by what the lawyers put in front of us. Endless ordinances needed to pass in order to put zoning laws on the books, to enact business licenses, collect franchise fees from the utilities, and so on, and so on. None were major policy issues that required much deliberation. Mainly we just had to put a structure of laws in place that were pretty cookie cutter, but necessary.

One issue did require judgment: how to move on adult entertainment. The decision was made to separate alcohol consumption from adult entertainment. Either drink, or see nudes, but not both at the same time. Of course, the existing establishments immediately challenged the move, as we expected, and the matter continues in ongoing litigation. The underlying constitutional issue is one most folks in Sandy Springs did not appreciate: the United States Supreme Court in its rulings protects adult entertainment as free speech. Much of the electorate simply expected the new city would just shut the places down. The press pounced on the new city without mercy. Its message was we were being provincial and that adult entertainment hurts nobody. The blogs went on for weeks

At the beginning, the decision was made by the council that the police department would start up in six months. A chief was employed early on, and, gradually,he assembled a superbly qualified force of some ninety officers, fully equipped for a full debut July 1, 2006. This was my birthday, and what a celebration I had riding in one of the cruisers, lights blinking, sirens at full force as the midnight hour launched the full force down Roswell Road. The new Sandy Springs contingent drove south on Roswell Road greeting the much smaller Fulton County group at its precinct as it drove north to mark the end of its responsibility in Sandy Springs.

Starting the fire department took longer. At the beginning we had hoped that the service Fulton County was providing under an agreement between city and county could continue. But it became evident that the county service was inadequate. One Saturday afternoon I was alerted to the fact that we had four stations in Sandy Springs and only two trucks operational. I called for reserve equipment from other stations and was informed they awaited repairs. Parts would be available in about two weeks. This was an impossible situation. Our bills from the county also reflected the number of personnel we had specified in the contract. Yet work records for the Fire Department as well as the Fulton police squad showed that the number present were often considerably less than the agreements specified and for which we were being billed. This led to the formation of the fire department by the first of January, 2007, a feat that was accomplished by the city manager and the fire chief he brought on board during the six-months interval.

Relations with the county were terrible. The squabbling went on and on about their not living up to the agreed terms for police and fire, and worst of all, a contingent of county commissioners announced they would sell the parks in Sandy Springs on the open market. The furor that followed engaged the entire metro press and political establishment. Even the *Atlanta Journal Constitution* (which had never favored the city of Sandy Springs) fulminated against the pettiness of the county proposal.

These parks in Sandy Springs had been more than paid for by our taxes in the past, so they belonged to us anyway. Indeed, our subsidies to the rest of the county had enabled purchase of parks outside of Sandy Springs. We were able to document that several of the parks were acquired by private funds or bequests, and, thus, were not even county expenditures. We also pointed out that if the county tried to sell the parks, there would be no buyers. Who would pay big bucks for parks that on our land-use map were shown for public use only? No buyer with good sense would take on a zoning battle to change public designation to private use.

The county commission was split three to four—three Republicans versus four Democrats, again along race lines. This split has been at the root of the commission's squabbles for years and inhibited rational considerations on many issues.

When the parks issue was brought up formally at the county commission, Commissioner Tom Lowe, representing our district, championed our cause and suggested selling the parks to us at a hundred dollars an acre. But the majority of the board insisted on an open-market sale. I focused on Commissioner Robb Pitts, a countywide commissioner. Perhaps I could change his mind. I documented for him the origin of all the parks in Sandy Springs, showing that they had been paid for by us, or donated, and succeeded in swinging him over completely. He now championed selling us the parks at one dollar an acre. (Some price would have to be paid to prevent the county from engaging in prohibited gratuities.) So now I had to bring together two commissioners who were ninety-nine dollars per acre apart. For six weeks the indecision went on and on. Finally Commissioner Lowe's hundred-dollar proposal carried the day with four votes.

While it was a frustrating process to watch, I really never had a grave fear of a different outcome. The whole situation was so preposterous that I knew it would eventually work out our way. The final outcome was even more beneficial to the city treasury: The Sandy Springs Society (a group of women who raise funds to support worthwhile activities in the community) came up with the donation of $16,600 to pay for the 166 acres of parks we acquired from the county. It was a delicious exclamation point to a silly vendetta.

Fulton County did not help itself in the parks fight with the wider community. A year after the incorporation of Sandy Springs all the remaining unincorporated area in North Fulton was also converted into new cities (Johns Creek and Milton.) On the south side of Fulton County the trend is still underway. The county with its bickering and mismanagement lost its status as the local service provider. Almost the entire county is contained within cities.

For a city that outsources all its major functions except public safety, the relationship between the private provider and the city of Sandy Springs is an area about which there is little guidance in the history of local government. Thus, we have had to learn as we progress in the relationship. Our contract is for a fixed amount and describes the services to be provided by the private firm. It does not define these services in specific output measures. Potholes are to be fixed, but nothing is said about how fast. Building permits are to be processed, but again, there are no guidelines about how quickly this is to be done. So, from a relationship that was built largely on trusting and a shaking of hands, the city will progress in years to come to contracts that are more definitive in terms of desired outcomes. This is not to say that the contracts will necessarily state the specific number of inputs (such as number of employees to be provided by the contract). The emphasis is instead on outputs—amount and quality of services provided. If a firm can achieve great outputs with fewer employees—more power to it, and no complaints. The purpose is not to monitor a company's profits, but rather to monitor the quality of its services.

Sandy Springs continues to host visitors from other states as well as other countries who are interested in our public/private partnership. There has been particular interest from Japan, where a strong push is on to reduce costs of local governments, and the public/private partnership of Sandy Springs is a model under strong consideration. Senator Vincent Fort, who had fought us to the end, declared at one point that "pigs will fly when Sandy Springs is a city!" Well, my office at city hall is now full of flying pigs. Representative Joe Wilkinson started the menagerie with battery-powered pigs that actually flap their wings, and soon everyone was finding similar novelties. The hilarious outcome of this is that Tokyo TV came to interview the new city about our novel public/private partnership, and I explained to them the congregation of pigs behind my desk. Lo and behold, when we received the tape of the Tokyo broadcast (which we could not understand), there I was, holding the flying pig with wings going full force.

There is nothing entirely routine about governing because the problems that arise are different from day to day. Together with the council, I deal with day laborers clamoring for jobs on Main Street and obstructing traffic, state laws that limit local revenues, and ever more complex environmental regulations impinging on all aspects of development. Problems on the front burner range from minute ones (size of allowable banners, tethering of dogs, and waterless urinals) to graver matters: a new city hall or a new recreation center, a dog park or a new soccer field? The variety of decisions, and people involved, is endless.

One hears a lot of talk of "public service" by elected officials. Usually one is lauded for such activity. The implication is that there is sacrifice involved in attending to the needs of the people. I think the public has it backwards. Elected officials are attracted by the challenge of the many decisions they must make. Nothing is ever quite the same. Nothing is ever boring. This is not a nine-to-five, watch-the-clock type of job. That's why we enjoy serving the people, and that is our true compensation for doing a job we enjoy.

So, as I near the end of my first term as the first mayor of Sandy Springs and look forward to a campaign for another four years, it is clear that forming the new city of Sandy Springs was a great idea, and our community is better off than it was. I am eager to continue to serve as Sandy Springs, our oh-so-fair city, continues to develop in its own unique and responsible way.

LaVergne, TN USA
29 March 2011
221925LV00001B/36/P